One Woman
One Faith
One Vision

ISBN: 978-0-615-24584-3

Foreword

Helen Duff Baugh was a woman ahead of her time. In a day when there were few women in Christian leadership—and even fewer in the forefront of evangelism—she had the boldness to follow God where He was leading in discovering opportunities to present the Gospel to others.

She was a visionary and an innovator—but Mrs. Baugh would have never described herself in that way. Instead, she would have said that her desire was to love, obey, and serve God completely. She trusted God in incredible ways, prayed, believed, and made herself available to Him. And God used her as she never could have imagined to make an impact for Him in hundreds of thousands of lives worldwide.

The story of Helen Duff Baugh amazes and inspires me. Her prayer life challenges me to seek God even more diligently. Her example of unfailing trust in God has been a wonderful model for me in times of uncertainty. And her willingness to share the unchanging Gospel with others in new and innovative ways, encourages me to trust God for His leading as we seek to reach new generations with His truth.

An ordinary woman with an extraordinary faith—that was Helen Duff Baugh. I pray that as you read her story, you will be reminded of what God can do through one life that is completely surrendered to Him.

Geneva Vollrath

President/CEO Stonecroft Ministries

Contents

Chapter 1

Missing the Boat

Helen Duff was nothing if not curious.

"Sir, what are you doing? If you don't mind me asking, that is."

The ship's mate turned from his task. Recognizing nine-year-old Helen with her two younger siblings in tow, he managed a brief smile.

"Well, Miss Duff, nothing for you to worry about. We're just taking the water temperature."

"Oh. Hmmm. Is that why we stop the ship so often? If you don't mind me asking, that is."

"No, I don't mind at all. I wish my children were as well-mannered as you, in fact. So…indeed, that is why we stop the ship so often, to read the water temperature. As I said before, there's nothing for you to worry about. We just want to make sure we're not traveling where too much ice can form in the water. We don't want to see any icebergs on this journey."

"Oh. Well." Helen seemed satisfied with that answer.

"But I tell you what. You've been such a good help to your mother, and you Duff children are all so well-behaved, I'd like you to go to the dining hall and ask for Mr. Clarkson. Tell Mr. Clarkson I'm giving you the Five Star Commendation for good conduct on board. He'll know what to do."

As the children enjoyed the tea and cookies provided by Mr. Clarkson, Helen asked, "Mr. Clarkson, is it bad for ice to be in the water with a boat?"

Mr. Clarkson's eyes grew wide. Then he looked away from the children. "Sometimes, miss. Sometimes indeed."

"Mama. *Mother.* Mama, are you all right?"

Mathilda Duff had just come off the *Scandinavian* with her four children in port at Halifax, Nova Scotia. The journey from Londonderry had often found Mathilda seasick and bedridden, along with eight-year-old Evangeline. Helen, her oldest, took charge of the younger two children.

Just at this moment, it looked as though Mathilda might faint again right in the middle of the gangplank. Nine-year-old Helen came to her right side to prop her up. Walter, a sturdy lad of five, did the same on Mathilda's left, while eight-year-old Evangeline held the hand of Olive, still a toddler.

Mathilda closed her eyes and steadied herself. She forced herself to breathe deeply. When she opened her eyes, her field of vision was clearing. She raised up to her full height, still allowing her children to assist her.

She looked again at the portside dock. The ship anchored there was already receiving its contents. Mathilda felt the sudden sting of tears. She choked out a sigh of relief, then allowed herself to wipe her eyes.

Helen pressed in closer to her mother, whispering now. "Mama! What is it?"

By all accounts of those who knew her, Mathilda Hamilton was a wonderful storyteller. Her light heart and vivid imagination brought life to almost any tale worth telling. Mathilda was also the artistic sort. Coming from a family of professional musicians, she easily held her own on the autoharp and organ.

Yet Mathilda had also lived through tragedy. She lost her parents when she was in her early teens. Her mother's sister raised Mathilda to adulthood. There, in her aunt's home, Mathilda learned of the love of Jesus. She felt the hand of God's providence on her life as never before and gave her life to full-time missions. She completed her college studies. Then, with great anticipation, Matilda applied to work as a missionary in Africa. Her character and qualifications were quite sound. However, the missions organizations to which Mathilda applied considered her health too delicate for the living conditions in Africa. They turned down her application for mission service. It was with her best interests in mind, they told her. Now what?

Sure that God had called her to tell others about Jesus, she looked for another opportunity to serve. Mathilda found an ad in a Liverpool newspaper for a short-term Bible study program in Ireland. She found the opportunity interesting enough to share it with her friend and roommate Sarah Palmer.

Mathilda and Sarah applied for and were accepted to study and work in the Christian Worker's Union in County Tyrone, Ireland. Full of enthusiasm, the girls made their journey.

The founder and director of the Irish Christian Worker's Union had already become a household name in northern Ireland, although not in the way his family had expected.

Tradition is a hard thing to break. You might as well try to break a horse without a halter, as the farmers of County Tyrone often said. But breaking tradition was exactly what Walter Duff was headed for.

By the 1890s in County Tyrone, Ireland, the Duff family had been wool and linen barons for two generations. The decade marked the peak of Oscar Wilde's literary productivity, and the births of many Irish children—including Michael Collins—who would become leaders of the Irish nationalist movement of the early 20th century. Guaranteed public education for the children of Ireland through age 14 became a reality. It seemed like Ireland was flexing muscles long waiting for exercise—and that God was preparing it for a fresh breeze of revival.

The windswept hills of County Tyrone were made for sheepherding, and the Duffs had been quick to make the most of it, building up a fine enterprise over the years. Walter, the youngest of three sons, was being groomed to take over the business. He'd already been off to university in England and had returned to take a real leadership role in the family venture. Walter was an aggressive young man, tall and long-faced. He and his brothers would make up the third generation to run their family business. But there was a wrinkle in all those long-laid plans.

Walter was a voracious reader. He especially liked nothing better on a Sabbath than to sit and read the paper. Catching up on the trends, checking on the wool futures, and relaxing were all allowed on a Sunday. The Duffs closed their mill so families could observe a real day of rest, no matter that the modern thought was beginning to say that Sabbath rest was a thing of the past. They had long been members of the church and tradition played its role in dictating Sabbath rest.

This particular Sunday was cold; the wind blew around the snug stone house. Walter lit a fire in his room and settled in to read the recent edition of the *British Christian Herald*. Among the articles, one in particular seemed to jump off the page and capture his attention: a sermon-in-print by a popular theologian named W. DeWitt Talmadge. Walter was familiar with this man, and was very interested in what he might have to say on the subject of heaven.

As he read, Walter became troubled. Not that Talmadge said things Walter thought were crazy notions about heaven. But in his heart, Walter was unsure if he would ever truly see heaven. What an amazing thought for someone who regularly went to church! However, according to this article, Walter had never actually done what God required to gain entrance to heaven: have a personal encounter with Jesus Christ.

Rather than stew about this unsettling thought, Walter took decisive action. He knelt down then and there and, in front of his fire, he spoke to God about the matter, committing his life to Jesus. When he sat back down in his chair, the old Walter was gone. And immediately, new ideas began to form in the back of his mind.

The next morning, just as he had done every morning since he could remember, Walter kissed his mother and said, "Mornin'," all around. As he and his brothers tucked into the food, Walter cleared his throat.

"Father, last night I became a Christian."

"Tut, tut, Walter. All Duffs are Christians. We attend church regularly and our firm gives heavily to support the church."

Walter's simple declaration, however, captured the attention of the rest of the family. All eyes were on him. "I know, Father, but last night God saved my soul!"

No one knew how to respond. It was a rather awkward moment.

Walter said no more right then, but as time went on his family became very aware that a change had come over him. He became driven to find out all he could about the Bible. He happened to overhear some men at the mill talking one day about a Bible study they held during their lunch hour—right there at the mill! They welcomed Walter into their group. He told them right away what had happened that Sunday night in his room. This group of men understood. It was his first opportunity to tell anyone outside his family about his new faith in Christ.

Once he'd opened his mouth, it seemed Walter couldn't close it. He began to tell others about his encounter with Jesus every chance he got. Walter began to hold meetings at the town hall. He'd speak anywhere he could. In only six months time, he'd taken the opportunity to lead hundreds of people to a personal relationship with Christ.

It became obvious to Walter that God had a different plan for him than staying at the mill. He knew God wanted him to become a full-time minister. When Walter told his family, tradition reared its head. His family tried every argument they could think of to convince him this couldn't possibly be the right thing for him to do.

"Walter, we need you in the family business," his father told him. "Stay with us. We'll cover the costs to keep two missionaries in China for your lifetime. Think of it, son: *two* workers in your stead, accomplishing *twice* what you might have done."

"Father, you don't understand. There would be no way for me to know what those two missionaries would be doing in China. God has called me—how could those men, even two of them, do what God has asked me to do? God has called *me* and I must go."

The elder Duff was not easily swayed. He tried another tactic. "Walter, if you insist on leaving the family business—especially after we have paid for an education for you to *be* in the family business—then you can count on nothing from us. No financial support whatsoever. No inheritance. Nothing."

Walter looked sadly at his father. "I hope you know that I love you...but I still must follow where God leads me."

Walter continued in his efforts to evangelize Ireland. He determined that seminary would be a good next step to help him fulfill God's call. Much to his surprise, once Walter entered seminary his father began sending money to pay for his training. Walter had to smile.

The days of training were like well-laid bricks in Walter's life. He became more sure of his biblical knowledge. He received more opportunities to preach and receive feedback on his style. He was able to wrestle with ideas and concepts with other young men in his classes. But what didn't change was his desire to tell other people about what Christ had done for him—for them. With each opportunity that was offered him, he prayerfully followed in obedience.

After seminary, Walter became frustrated that he felt his efforts were "not enough." He needed more "Walters" to do this big job God has asked him to do! "God, how can I do such a big job? How can I get it all done? I need some wisdom, here!"

Walter was not surprised to have a great idea pop into his head. Why not teach others what seemed to come naturally to him? Why not pass on his passion for evangelism to the very people whose hearts were soft toward the Savior?

So Walter began to train the young men and women who gave their lives to Christ in his meetings. He designed a course to teach them Bible knowledge. But Walter knew that knowledge alone would not get things done. He also gave his students opportunities to do the work alongside him.

Walter's brainstorm was bigger than training only. Each time he'd go into a new area to preach, he would walk around and look for the largest home in the area available to rent. In an idea very revolutionary for his time, Walter began renting these houses with fifteen or more bedrooms. Then he would fill them with the young people he was ready to train. He brought in highly skilled Bible teachers who held classes every morning and afternoon. Every evening these young people would use any means they could—horses, buggies, bicycles, or their own two feet—to scatter throughout the surrounding area and hold meetings. Schools, lodges. and town halls would fill with people eager to hear what these young men and women had to say.

By the late 1890s, Walter's idea was known as the Irish Christian Worker's Union. But his vision didn't stop there. One by one, he bought up large old tents until he had eight: one for each county in northern Ireland. These were used to hold outdoor meetings when a building couldn't be secured in an area. From his travels and the work of his students—hundreds of young men and women over the years—"Walter Duff" became a household name. The students he trained would go on to be ministers and missionaries on every continent in the world. By being obedient to God's calling, God had given Walter so far greater an impact than if he'd agreed with his father to send two missionaries to China in his place!

Even in the midst of doing God's work, God had more in store for Walter. Not long after Mathilda Hamilton and her friend Sarah Palmer traveled to County Tyrone to work with Walter's Christian Worker's Union, Mathilda caught Walter's eye. Upon meeting Mathilda, Walter immediately noticed the deep love she had for Jesus. This girl was not afraid to speak out. Her brown eyes sparkled as she told of how she first met her Savior. Walter was quite taken with her love for ministry, but he was a man, after all, and he also became aware of her dark brown hair, her quick smile, tiny figure and her Irish wit each time he was near her. She had a distinct charm, and his attraction to her was immediate. Before too long, they became engaged.

On March 1, 1901, Walter took Mathilda Hamilton as his bride. After a quick honeymoon to Loch Lomond, Scotland, they returned to Ireland to begin working together as a true team. God had large plans for them, as this was the time of great revival in the British Isles. Walter and the other Union missionaries sometimes held meetings attended by as many as five thousand people. This time of spiritual awakening was so tremendous that someone said, "There is hardly a person in all Northern Ireland who cannot explain the simplicity of the grace of God."

During this time of training and sending out Union evangelists, Walter and Mathilda had four children of their own: Helen, Alexandra (later known as Evangeline), Walter, Jr., and Olive. Mathilda's health proved to be fragile. Often during these years, she was confined to bed. However, her love for her Savior and her children never allowed her illness to diminish her impact as a mother. Her children would gather around her bed in the evenings and Mathilda would read to them from the Bible or books about missionaries. After reading, the children would beg her, "Now you tell it, Mother!" Mathilda would then bring a perhaps dry story to life with animation and enticing details. These evenings provided Matihilda's children with some of their fondest memories from their young lives.

When Mathilda was feeling well, she would take long walks with her children, helping them to gain an eye for God's great creation. She would point out details they might otherwise have missed: the texture of a tree's bark, the fine veins in a dragonfly's wings. She taught them to be able to identify flowers and trees, birds and animals. Together they enjoyed fresh air and exercise and the love of God as He showed Himself in creation.

Mathilda also poured her great love for music into her young children. Her father had been a church choir director and her sister was a famous singer, known to others as "the sweet singer of Londonderry." The Duff family spent many evenings gathered around their family organ. Mathilda played as she led her family in singing hymns and folk tunes, passing on to her children the passion for music her parents had given her.

The young pastors and missionaries trained in the Christian Worker's Union wrote often to Walter and Mathilda to tell of the great things they were watching God do all around the globe. Many had felt a call to serve in the United States, and had moved there to continue in their ministries. Their letters often begged the Duffs to join them in their work in the States. "The opportunities are multiplied here," they would write. Walter always refused to go, sure that God's purpose for him was still in Ireland. Over time, however, he developed a strange stirring when he read of an invitation to this far country.

Walter tried to be reasonable. He was nearly forty years old. Surely that was far too old to be making such a drastic change in his life and ministry. Try as he might to find reasons *not* to go, Walter could only come up with weighty reasons *to* go. After much deliberation and prayers together, he and Mathilda decided that God was indeed leading them to make a move across the ocean to the United States.

The custom of the time dictated that Walter go ahead of his family to find work and a place to live. Once he'd established himself, he would send for the family to join him. How difficult it was for Walter and Mathilda to separate! They had never really been apart in all their married life. Walter felt awful leaving his wife behind with the children, no matter how capable he knew her to be. Even providing a servant to help with the children would not alleviate the burden Mathilda would have to bear. Such a great distance would lie between them, and how long would it take for him to be ready to send for them? But even with all his heartache, he knew God was leading them to this new place, and he had to follow.

Walter's ship took less than four days to reach New York City. An Irish pastor in Minneapolis helped Walter find a position in International Falls, Minnesota, at the Baptist church there. A church across the border in Fort Francis, Ontario, also was without a pastor, so Walter found himself pastoring two small churches in two countries. He agreed to preach in International Falls on Sunday mornings, and then row himself across the Rainy River to preach Sunday evenings in the Canadian church. Settled with a paying job, he quickly found a house in International Falls large enough for his family.

Walter then took on the task of booking passage for his family to join him. He found what he thought was the perfect opportunity to provide a smooth trip for his wife and four youngsters. A brand new ship was being built right in Belfast, and the stir surrounding it was growing as the vessel neared completion. It was reported to be the world's fastest ship, "unsinkable," and the grandest, most opulent ocean liner ever built. It would sail in April 1912; perfect timing for his family.

Walter was sure his family would have a safe, comfortable crossing as he booked third class tickets for them on the *Titanic.*

The days passed slowly for Mathilda as she waited to hear from Walter with news of a job and the arrangements he'd made for the family's passage to America. Two months turned to four, and four dragged on for what seemed to be forever. Mathilda was thrilled when the letter arrived from Walter with the plans for their move. She set to work packing and planning what they would need and what they would leave behind. April could just not get there fast enough for Mathilda.

However, February brought some bad news. A coal strike in England caused all large ships, whose coal consumption was great, to delay departure dates. The *Titanic*, whose launch would be from Southampton, England, would not launch until the strike was over.

Mathilda was determined not to be separated from her Walter any longer. And, it turned out, so was Walter. He wired her the short message, "Change plans. Sail from Londonderry." That settled it—and Mathilda was so relieved. This way she would not have to travel alone with her children from Ireland to Southampton to catch the original ship; they could leave right from Ireland. Mathilda cancelled their tickets on the *Titanic* and made new reservations for them on a steamship called the *Scandinavian*. The *Scandinavian* was less than two-thirds the size of the *Titanic* and not as finely appointed, but it would have to do.

The young family was a bit disappointed to miss sailing on the *Titanic* along with some of the world's wealthiest and most influential people. It would have been marvelous! But the change in plans did not dampen their joy in being able to unite all the sooner with Walter. They boarded the newly painted ship and located their quarters. The family was a bit taken aback by the room's tiny size, yet they found it comfortable.

At sea, the size of the cabin did not matter as seasickness set in. Mathilda and Evangeline, almost eight at their departure, spent nearly the entire passage in the cabin, ill. Helen was left to watch the other two children. Mathilda was so grateful for Helen's ability to look out for the small ones and keep them away from the cabin while she was sick. The children were given free run of the ship, racing on the deck and having countless adventures. The crew and other passengers kept an eye on them, and found them to be friendly, charming children.

Mathilda hoped her trip across the ocean would be as swift as her husband's. After seven days with still no sign of land, Mathilda wondered if she would ever stop being seasick.

Even more unsettling, right in the middle of the Atlantic, the ship began to make frequent full-stops. The children reported to Mathilda that the crew were acting very worried and doing strange things each time they stopped. When the children questioned the sailors, they answered that they were checking water temperature to watch out for icebergs.

The boat made excruciatingly slow progress. One day the engines stopped again, but this time they did not resume after the usual time. When the children asked the crew about the stop, they found out disappointing news. The coal strike had caused the ship to leave port without their full supply of coal. All the stopping and starting had used up their fuel! They were dead in the water until a refueling ship could reach them.

Fourteen days into their journey, the small ship finally reached its first scheduled landfall at Halifax, Nova Scotia. It was only then that Mathilda learned of the *Titanic*'s sinking.

The news of the *Titanic*'s tragic end overwhelmed Mathilda, as did the sight of Halifax in response to the disaster. The whole of Halifax was draped in black in mourning over the loss. Coffins were stacked in rows on the docks, ready to be loaded on two ships being sent out to recover the bodies of the victims.

Though the *Scandinavian* left port before the *Titanic*, the larger and faster boat had nearly overtaken the smaller ship when it hit an iceberg and sank. The captain of Mathilda's ship had learned of the *Titanic*'s fate on his new wireless during their trip across the Atlantic. For that reason, he decided to make frequent iceberg checks and take his time crossing. The small ship passed within three hundred miles of the spot where the *Titanic* went down.

The Duff family made their way down the gangplank and into Halifax proper. Along the way, Mathilda heard more harrowing details. Less than a third of the souls who sailed on the Titanic, around 710 of the about 2,200 people on board, survived the tragedy. Many of the twenty lifeboats on board were not even full when they launched from the ship. Only a small number of the Irish immigrants in third class were able to get to the top deck to board the lifeboats.

As Mathilda put together the story of the "unsinkable" *Titanic*, she was deeply shaken. Had she followed their original plan, chances were great that she and her four dear children would be dead! Thank God that He had prompted Walter and her to reunite their family earlier than planned!

Mathilda looked at her four children one by one: Helen. Evangeline. Walter, Jr. Olive. She knelt and gathered them all into her arms.

There was no coincidence here. It was clear as day that God had spared them.

Mathilda shivered as she wondered what marvelous things must be planned for her little family.

Chapter 2

Sculpting the Next Generation

A new world awaited Mathilda and her children—but not until she could pass through customs in Boston. Mathilda was exhausted from her longer-than-expected journey and the blow from the devastating news about the *Titanic.* But dry land felt so good under their feet. The children danced a small jig until Mathilda shushed them in the long line shuffling forward to the customs officer.

The officer they reached had already had a long day himself. Helen took note that he was not very patient, nor very nice to Mathilda as she handed him her papers. Glancing at her papers, he laughed cruelly at their long, traditional Irish names. "Think you're royalty, do ya?" he jabbed.

Mathilda had to look away to hide the tears that sprang to her eyes. She just couldn't hold up any longer. She needed her husband. She needed rest. She needed some help, here!

Immediately the customs officer felt terrible for hurting this young mother, obviously tired from her crossing, trying valiantly to corral four lively children. He grabbed his stamp and pounded it on her papers. "Lady, you got an honest face. Go on through."

Gratefully, Mathilda nodded her thanks to the officer, not trusting her voice to speak. She gathered up her papers, her children and all their bags and walked to the heart of Boston in search of a hotel room. No matter where she went the word was the same—full! At last, one kind desk manager allowed Mathilda and her children to sleep in his lobby. The next morning, a bit worse for the wear, the young family boarded their train for Minnesota. No matter how tired or travel-worn they were, they were glad to be on the train. It was at last the final leg of the journey before reaching their new home.

Walter was ecstatic at the reunion with his family! As they got off the train, he grabbed each child in turn and hugged them as though trying to make up for several months of loneliness and separation. Even though it was not deemed proper in the day, Walter could not contain his emotions. He cried as he held each child and Mathilda. God's mercy was clear. His family was with him and now they could go ahead with whatever God had planned.

The adjustment to life in Minnesota was hard for Mathilda. She was used to dense urban living. In rural Minnesota, there were trees and lakes and forests and rivers and more trees! The one thing she clung to as comfort was that their house was in town, small as the town might be with its population of 1,000. A private Irish woman, Mathilda also had to adjust to the outspoken and, to her views, crude Swedish immigrants who inhabited International Falls. In time she learned to love them and appreciate the very differences that made them unique, and made it a point to remind the children of the same.

The new place and culture brought many adventures to the Duff family. The churches held frequent picnics and walks among the deep forests. The children loved the chance to run and play in vacant lots in town. So many new things to taste and touch and see!

Not only were the Swedish immigrants a whole new culture to the Duffs, but also they daily rubbed shoulders with the Native American Indians who lived in the area. Tall and thin, agile and friendly, these native peoples were fascinating to the children, and they learned much by watching them.

In a small town such as International Falls, friendships became very important. The unmarried minister at the Episcopalian church became a close friend. When the Duffs moved to town, he was immediately drawn to their warmth. The chance to be connected to a family was more than he could resist. This lonely minister spent many evenings at the Duff home, and he would often bring fresh maple syrup as a gift. He spent time with the children, teaching them how to roll bits of maple syrup in the snow, pulling and shaping it into scrumptious candy.

Mathilda's gift for organization proved useful in raising her children. She assigned duties to each child according to their age and ability. Early in life, Helen, Evangeline, and Walter, Jr. could make their own beds, set the table, put away their clothes, wash dishes, and carry wood in for the fire.

The children knew without a doubt that their mother's rules were to be obeyed! She was the disciplinarian in the family, although none of the children ever tried to cross their father. Both Mathilda and Walter knew from Scripture that God asks obedience from His children. They in turn, tried to train their children to obey. Talking, spanking, revoking privileges, all were methods they used to rein in the Scotch-Irish temperaments bred into their children! Helen often felt that she took the punishment for all the children's naughtiness. She was often sent by her father to check on Walter, Jr. He would say to her, "Go see what Walter is doing and tell him to stop it!" No matter the discipline at the time, the children came to realize that learning to obey their parents taught them how to obey God.

Mathilda was ever watchful of her children's education. That first winter in a new country, she began what came to be known as an "evening reader." While the children did dishes after dinner, they would each take a turn reading. Mathilda picked books by Charles Dickens as well as the Scottish author Robert Louis Stevenson. How the children loved the exciting tales read out loud to one another in the warm, steamy kitchen. The Duffs were, indeed, a well-read family.

Helen learned early in her life that her parents had very vital relationships with God. If she would get up in the middle of the night to wander to the bathroom, a glance in her parent's room would find her mother sitting up in bed. Lamplight shone on her face as she read the Bible in her lap. She'd found that the only time she could spend in quiet prayer and reading was after all her brood was in bed asleep! Her husband had time each day as he worked to spend time with the Lord alone, but a mother of five found her time at night. Little did Mathilda know the impression she was making on her young children. The picture of their mother's quiet life of faith would stay with and influence her children the rest of their lives.

Winter brought many joys, including the anticipation of a new baby. The other Duff children were beside themselves waiting for the arrival of the first American Duff. Haldane was born on May 21, 1913 in a small rural hospital only blocks from the Duffs' home. In those days, women and babies stayed in the hospital for at least a week or two when a new baby came. So, Helen dutifully walked the rest of the children to the hospital on a daily visit. When Mathilda and Haldane were finally able to come home, everyone was ready. What a happy day!

Spring progressed to summer and summer to fall, and Walter began to be alarmed by Mathilda's health. The winter in Minnesota had been a severe one, and Mathilda had not responded easily to it. She had often been unable to get out of bed. As the days progressed, she seemed to get worse rather than better. Evangeline and Helen, just nine and ten years old, took on most of the household responsibilities. A great sadness and quiet settled over the once lively home in International Falls as each one began to fear Mathilda might die.

Walter decided it was time to act. He began to question everyone he saw, "Where in the United States is there a place with a climate that is mild like our Ireland?" Over and over again, he was told to check into the Pacific Northwest. Church members in the Fort Francis church helped him get in contact with an

Irish pastor in Oregon. Through this contact, Walter was able to preach before a church in Portland that was searching for a pastor. In the spring of 1914, Walter packed up his family and their belongings and moved to Portland to become the pastor of Calvary Baptist Church. It seemed that nature itself had turned out to greet them—flowers bloomed everywhere they looked. Large roses bloomed along each sidewalk, in colors more spectacular than any they could remember seeing before. By the fall they were all settled into Portland and Walter's second American church.

Walter's church was located about twelve blocks from the family's new home. Each Sunday they made quite a picture as they paraded the route to and from Calvary Baptist.

The walk was good for all of them. It allowed all the "Sunday morning rush" to settle out of them. Walter and Mathilda, followed by Helen, Evangeline, Walter, Jr., Olive, and Haldane in his pram, strolled the twelve blocks to church.

The weather in Oregon was all Walter had hoped for, but the climate in his church was not. The Duffs quickly became friends with the people in Calvary Baptist, but no amount of urging by Walter could get any of his congregation interested in telling others about Jesus. Clearly, he felt the whole of Portland was in a "spiritual slump."

Walter decided that he must reach out to those who needed to hear the Gospel, even if no one from his church joined him. So one day in 1918, Walter grabbed his son, Walter, Jr. and they headed off to take the streetcar to the downtown section of Portland. Walter told his son, "Look around you, son. These streets are filled with men who need to know about Jesus. We've got to find a way to tell them. Let's you and I look around here for a building we can rent so we can hold meetings—"

"Like you did back in Ireland, Father?" Walter asked.

"Yes, son, like I did back in Ireland. We'll have our services and give out literature...I'm sure it will be just what the men of Portland need."

After looking around, they settled on a building on the corner of Alder and 3rd streets. Within weeks, Walter had dubbed the place "Hope Hall," and the ministry he began there grew quickly. Every Sunday, after preaching at Calvary, Walter would take the streetcar, usually joined by his family, and hold services at Hope Hall, afternoon and evening.

Just when life looked as if it was settling into a calm routine, Mathilda again became ill. She was not able to get out of bed, but did her best to care for her family from there. But no matter how much rest she got, Mathilda just grew worse. Walter had no choice but to take her see a doctor.

When they returned home, Walter was carrying Mathilda. He did not stop to say anything to the children, who had been waiting anxiously for the return of their parents. Wide-eyed, they silently watched their father carry their mother up the stairs to her bed. Fear gripped every small heart because they had seen the fear in their mother's eyes. After Walter had fixed some tea and taken it up to Mathilda, he finally returned to the children.

"Let's go to the kitchen and have a little talk." The family, still quiet, gathered around the large kitchen table. Walter cleared his throat. He reached up and rubbed his eyes before looking at each child in turn. They all thought they might burst if he didn't tell them what had filled their mother's eyes with such fear! But none of them dared ask. Father would tell them in time.

"The doctor has told us your mother has what is called 'consumption.' He said she is very bad and will only get worse. He said she will surely die, and that this will happen fairly soon. Your mother is very fearful, because her mother died of consumption...so she is very afraid of what the doctor said."

Walter paused to let this sink in to the children. When he spoke again, his tears were flowing freely. "However," he said with emphasis, "that doctor does not know Jesus. We do! So we are going to pray. We are going to believe. We are going to ask Jesus to heal your mother—to spare her life. We are going to trust Jesus to do what we know He can do."

The little family knelt there in the kitchen and began to pray. Their tears fell as they asked God to restore the life of the woman they loved. They prayed as rain fell outside and the day became dark, and the rain stopped. But still they prayed. At last Walter got up from his knees and lit the lamps in the house. He helped his children off to bed. As he tucked each one in, he told them, "We know that Jesus hears our prayers. We will watch and see God's hand at work."

It took weeks for Mathilda to regain her strength, but regain it she did. Finally she was well enough that she was able to join the rest of her family in the kitchen for a meal. And what a celebration the family held that night! With grateful hearts, they thanked God for restoring Mathilda's health. With loud cheers they rejoiced that she was still with them—and learned an invaluable lesson about the power of prayer.

One thing Walter longed for was that his children should not be raised totally in the city. If he could at least get them to the suburbs where they could have some room to roam, he knew it would be much better for them. After living in the city for about two years, he pooled his resources with two other minister friends and together they bought some land. This land was next to Chautauqua Park in Gladstone, Oregon. The setting was mostly rural, with trees and a great view of the park. Walter's two acres were in the middle of the parcel. He hired a friend to help him build his family a new home.

Everyone pitched in to help build the house. It was a lively several months as children moved in and out among the builders. They helped by carrying boards and shingles, handing hammers and nails to the skilled workers. The children were given priceless, hands-on lessons in construction, responsibility, and teamwork that Walter knew would prove valuable as they grew older. With so many hands helping, the house went up quickly. It seemed like no time at all, and the young family was moved in and enjoying their home. With great joy, the family named their new home "Duffmont."

As it turned out, the other two ministers never did get around to building on their properties. The Duff children had run of all six acres—and run they did. Their years at Duffmont were happy ones. The family resumed their habit of walking together among the trees and identifying plants and animals. They learned to know each bird by its song. And they learned to know their Creator better by knowing the things He created, down to the scents of the various blooming bushes and shrubs. The small children would cry out with excitement, "Look at that squirrel! His mouth is full of something!" Or, "Which kind of flower is this? Is this a trillium?" "Oh, I love that flower!"

In the summers, Chautauqua Park hosted varied programs for only ten cents admission. The Duff children loved to attend. It was easy for them to get there—they ran across their yard and into the park! However, Mathilda and Walter were stern with their instructions each time the children left for a program: "Once you arrive at the lake, before you go into the auditorium, go out the front gate and pay your ten cents. Then you may go back in and enjoy the show." Not one of the children ever considered going in without paying. The honesty of their parents was being ingrained into the children, and it was never an option in their young minds to be otherwise.

The years at Duffmont also were a time of growing ministry for Mathilda. She was a gifted teacher but, since she'd left Ireland she had no chance to teach anyone besides her children. Mathilda began to teach Bible classes around Portland and Salem. It was not an easy thing for her to do with five young children. Each Tuesday she would rise early and get the children dressed and fed. Then she would walk a mile and a half to the streetcar line for the ride to the city. After teaching her class, she made the trip in reverse. This process took Mathilda most of the day, so Walter, ever in support of her service, hired a housekeeper to help her out. This gave her such peace of mind knowing that the children were cared for in her absence.

Mathilda also used to love to use the early gospel tracts that were becoming available. Her heart for evangelism caused her to see so many needs around her. When she could not speak directly to a need, she would leave a tract. When shopping or traveling, Mathilda always left a calling card—a gospel tract left in a strategic place. She was always ready to do anything she felt she could to advance the Gospel of Jesus Christ, then, and for the rest of her life.

Walter preached to many people over the years, but his heart was always watchful for the chance to lead one of his own children to the Lord. Every morning he led his family in devotions. After breakfast, Walter read from the Bible. Then father, mother and each child knelt by their chairs to pray. Once his children had committed their lives to the Lord, Walter allowed them to pray as well. Helen's chance came when she was twelve. She finally understood that the sacrifice of Jesus was for *her*—Helen. She gave her life to the Lord in a heartfelt prayer of dedication. Thereafter, she prayed every morning with her parents and brothers and sisters.

After their time of prayer one morning, the four oldest Duff children hurried off to school. They arrived, happy enough, only to be told they were tardy! All of the children were marched off to see the principal. Miss Dimmick gave them a stern little lecture about the importance of promptness and the downward slope of tardiness. She sent the children to their classrooms, but told them in no uncertain terms to bring a note from their parents the next day.

That night around the dinner table, four anxious children told in excited voices just what had happened that day when they arrived at school. Their father nodded and said quietly, "I'll write the note you need. Don't worry. Take it with you tomorrow and give it to Miss Dimmick. The note will do the trick."

In the morning after family prayers, the children were a bit less excited to head to school. But they dutifully marched to Miss Dimmick's office and Helen handed her the note their father had written.

"Is this your excuse?" asked Miss Dimmick. She pursed her lips as she looked at the children.

Four little heads nodded yes, and quietly watched her as she opened the note and read. They could not believe their eyes. As she read, a smile spread across Miss Dimmick's face. None of the children could ever remember seeing her *smile*. What could that note have said? She looked at the children and said, "Alright, children. You may go on to your classrooms."

The children were nearly bursting by the time dinner arrived and they could ask, "Father, what did you write in the note you sent with us today?" "Yeah, what did you put in that excuse? It made Miss Dimmick *smile*." That just didn't happen. The children shook their heads in bewilderment.

A smile tugged at the corner of Walter's mouth as he said, "Well, I told her the truth. I just wrote, 'Please excuse our children for being late. Our clock told a lie.'"

Throughout her teen years, Helen's desire was to tell others about the joy and peace they could have through knowing God. One day she and a friend were walking home from high school. Somehow the conversation turned to Jesus. Helen carefully explained how her friend could become a Christian. Her friend turned to look into Helen's eyes and said, "Can I do this now?" So Helen and her friend stopped right where they were and prayed. "Lord Jesus, please forgive my sins," Helen's friend prayed. "Come into my life. I want to know you!" Helen was thrilled and came home from school that day, bursting with the news of being able to lead her friend to Christ.

Helen's faith grew as she did. But her sense of humor and Irish wit also grew. Helen was a child who loved fun and loved to joke and make people laugh. After several years living at Duffmont, Walter built another house on their property. Again the children were called upon to be part of the work crew. Walter felt nothing could prepare his children for life than hands-on experience. During the days, all would be hard at work. In the evenings, Walter would light a big bonfire using the scraps from the day's building. The workers and family would gather around the fire, swapping stories and relaxing together. One evening one of the younger workers named Lake Smith was standing near Helen at the bonfire. She noticed he seemed to be glancing her way a lot. Finally, he looked directly at her through the smoky haze and boldly said, "Helen, you're a good looking gal."

Helen, about 15 at the time, was startled by Lake's frank statement. However, she was in possession of her tremendous wit and quickly fired back at him, "I wish I could say that about you!"

Not missing a beat, Lake, smiling sweetly, replied, "You could if you could lie like I can!" Everyone around the fire had a great laugh over this exchange.

Although his family and his life were moving along smoothly, Walter could not ignore that something within him was shifting. The church in Portland was merely maintaining, while downtown, things were happening. When he preached there, people responded with hungry hearts to God. They wanted to know Jesus, and they wanted to know about God's Word. Walter had a decision to make. He wanted with all his heart to be in evangelistic ministry again, but how could he do that with no financial base? He had a growing family, after all. Leaving the church would mean leaving a salary. It might mean another move.

Walter and Mathilda again set their hearts to prayer. For all the good reasons they could come up with *not* to leave the security of the pastorate, they kept coming back to the one small reason of "calling." Both of them agreed. It was clear to them that God was calling them to evangelistic ministry. Walter resigned his pastorate at Calvary Baptist Church. Obedience to God seemed to him, and to Mathilda, the only choice they could make.

Walter accepted a pastorate in a small congregation on Portland's east side. For two years he continued to work downtown at Hope Hall while leading the tiny church in town. In return for opening the church that had been closed for years, the state Baptist Committee agreed to let the Duffs live in the small parsonage and give them a $20 a month stipend. His family was covered and Walter believed God would do the rest.

In addition to his other duties, Walter began to hold meetings up and down the coast through Washington, Oregon, and British Columbia. He started to include the children in his work. One by one, each of them joined the traveling group. Walter was never big on formal education, and so to him it was no big deal to pull the children out of school to go with him. Helen, the oldest, was first to go with him. Noting his eldest daughter's gifts for teaching and evangelism, Walter would frequently ask Helen to come to the platform and explain the teaching chart he was using in his presentation.

Mathilda did not mind her children traveling with their father. But she so wanted her children to finish school that she found reasons for each one of them to stay with her. It was her way of assuring that each of her children finished high school. However long it took, the children did complete their schooling. Evangeline was nearly twenty before she finished, due to the long trips with her father.

Walter laid a very clear foundation in each of his children's lives. His passion for evangelism spilled over to his children. He taught them that they each must be in some kind of Christian work to be fully in God's will. He felt each of them must have the skills needed, whether they were boys or girls, to do the same work that consumed him. Due to his training, each of his children could play hymns, lead songs, and preach.

Mathilda joined Walter's efforts by training the children to play numerous musical instruments. She taught them duets and trios for instruments and voice. As soon as the children were old enough, each of them joined in full-time evangelistic work, completely trained and equipped.

The Duff children were instilled with a love for God, a deep joy in prayer, and a great desire to serve Him. Bottom line, Walter had taught the children that if they were not serving the Lord in some way, they probably were out of God's will for their lives.

This principle struck a deep chord with Helen, especially. She had given her life to the Lord at twelve and had since dedicated her life to full-time service, wherever that might take her.

Chapter 3

On Tour

Late in life, Helen Duff Baugh would write of her experience as a young itinerant evangelist with her sisters in the Duff Sisters Gospel Trio, "Many and varied were our experiences in rural America. But always one thought was uppermost in our minds. In each community there were people—fathers, mothers, young people—who did not know our Lord Jesus in a personal way. Our one desire was to present Christ in such an attractive manner that those without Christ could not resist His love. Hundreds of people made their reservations for Heaven through hearing how to do it at our meetings."

There is no question Helen shared her father's passion for country folk. Walter's pastorates were in cities, but his heart had always returned to rural areas. He knew that in these areas many small churches were forced to close their doors for lack of their ability to afford a pastor. He passed on to his children his love for rural churches. Walter had asked the deacons at his city church to cover the Wednesday night Bible studies. That left him free to travel to country churches through the week and still allowed him to be back at the city church to preach on Sundays.

When he returned from holding meetings in a small church, he told stories of his experiences. Gathered around the dinner table with his family, he would say, "You should have seen the joy in those people's faces. They were so appreciative of getting some Bible teaching. Their church closed five years ago."

Helen looked at her father, eyes wide. "But why, Father? I didn't think churches ever closed."

"Children, that's the sad truth. There just aren't enough men or women in ministry to serve all these small towns. There are many churches closed and locked up all over rural America." Walter got a faraway look in his eye. "It's really a crime. There ought to be something we can do..."

Helen thought her heart would explode! She felt every word her father had said. She knew God was calling her to become a missionary to rural America. As soon as she was old enough, Helen began to travel with her father on his trips into rural areas.

In the days before television and radio, few people had the chance to hear Bible teaching. But many people came to hear the traveling Bible teacher. Through his classes, hundreds of people were given the opportunity to gain a solid biblical foundation that they otherwise would never have received. Walter had asked Mathilda to make some large charts to illustrate his messages. Without warning, he'd often say during his meetings, "Helen, why don't you come up here and explain this chart?" Up she'd pop and go carefully to the platform and put in plain words the meaning of the visual aid. Before she left the stage, Helen gave her father a big grin.

The foundation that Walter and Mathilda had laid in teaching their children—instructing them to play many instruments and sing, taking them along as Walter held his own evangelistic meetings, pouring into them their concern for those who didn't know the Savior—made it natural, as the girls reached their late teens, for them to present Christian musical presentations with a message. They all felt a great urgency to tell others about Jesus and to do so without delay. Walter, Jr. often traveled with the girls as their evangelist, the girls providing the music. But more and more, their brother was off holding his own meetings.

Helen and her sisters began to "dream big." One day, Olive, Evangeline, and Helen approached their father. They knew of a community near theirs that had no church. "Father, over in

Park Place there's that lovely church that is locked up. No one uses it at all," Evangeline started.

Helen quickly chimed in, "We were thinking that we'd like to do a Sunday school there."

"What do you think? May we have your permission to try, Father?" Olive finished.

Walter rubbed his chin as he thought a bit. But as soon as his girls had begun to ask, he knew what his answer would be. "I think it's a splendid idea. You'll need to find who owns the building and ask their permission. If you get their permission, you'll have to clean the place and make it ready to hold guests. Can you do all that?'

Three eager teen girls said, "Yes!" They immediately set off for the small town to talk with the "powers that be." Finally one person involved in the conversation said, "Why not let them go ahead with their idea? They are only young people. What harm can they do?"

The girls were thrilled. The church was not in bad shape, so the building was ready in no time to receive guests. The girls decided the best way to advertise their Sunday school was to go door to door. Off they set, calling on each home in the small town. Each person was invited to come to the Sunday school.

And come they did! The church building was filled with adults as well as children. One highlight of this particular Sunday school was that the Duff's family friend Lake Smith attended. (He was the young man who teased with Helen around the bonfire at Duffmont.) Lake became a Christian at their Sunday school and later taught the men's Bible class there.

The Duff girls didn't stop there. They found another church—but this one was in horrible shape. All the windows had been vandalized and were gone. The front door was hanging off its hinges. Inside the girls found the pulpit still in place, and the large pulpit Bible lying open on it, the pages whipping open and closed in the breeze. The church had been abandoned many years before, and it appeared that no one in the community had taken any time to try to look after it. The girls looked at each other and knew this church should be their next project.

Helen approached her father. "Father, we've located another church…but this one is in pretty bad shape. We'd sure like to check around about fixing it up with the thought of holding some meetings there."

Looking at her over his paper, Walter noticed his other daughters behind Helen, hands clasped in anticipation of what he might say. "Mmm, sounds interesting. Are you here for my permission?'

Helen turned a little red as she glanced at her sisters. "Well, yes we are."

Walter nodded, but didn't say anything. He kept his eyes on his first-born.

Helen hurried on as she said, "We also wondered if you might give us a dollar for some gas money so we could go check into opening up this church." There. She'd said it.

In those days, gas was fifteen cents a gallon. But also in those days, a dollar was a lot of money. The girls waited as their father shifted in his chair and reached for his wallet. "I can think of a lot of ways to spend a dollar, but not too many of them quite so good. I'll pray for you as you go after this next ministry." The girls each thanked him and rushed off to buy gas and head out to try to open this poor, dilapidated church.

The girls had to ask several people in the small town about the church before finding someone who could give them any direction at all. They were sent to see a lawyer named Lauterette who was property manager for the building. His secretary escorted the young ladies into Mr. Lauterette's office where the girls explained to him their idea for using the building.

Pulling on his whiskers thoughtfully, Mr. Lauterette said, "Well, now, I think that might be a good use for that old eyesore of a building. But I'm just not sure it's safe for anyone to be in there. Certainly not safe for a whole crowd of people. Could be that old place would come right down around your ears!"

The girls were sure he was trying to tell them "No" without hurting their feelings, when the lawyer continued. "However, I'll tell you what. If you can find two carpenters who could tell you if that building is safe enough for your meetings, then I'll give you my permission to use it. How's that sound?"

The girls, all grins, said it sounded just fine to them. Nearly giddy with the near-yes, they left Mr. Lauterette's office in search of carpenters.

The first man they encountered walking down the street was a bit startled to be stopped by three young girls. "Excuse me," Evangeline said. "Would you happen to be a carpenter?"

Laughing, the man said, "I sure am. How did you know?"

Helen, all business, said, "Oh we didn't. But we are looking for carpenters to give us their informed opinion about a building." She pointed across the street. "Do you see that building down over there? It's in pretty bad condition. But we need to know if you, as a carpenter, think it would hold a large group of people and not collapse on them."

The man shook his head, and smiled. "I've been in that building—long time ago, of course. I've seen how it was put together. I don't think you could fit enough people into it to get it to collapse."

"Oh, thank you for your time! We really appreciate it!" the girls called to him as they set off to find anther carpenter.

Before long, another man was coming toward them along the street. When asked if he was a carpenter, he told the girls he was. "What do you want me to build you?" he eagerly asked.

"We don't want anything built," Olive replied. "But we do need an expert opinion about that old church over there. Would you consider that building of sound structure?"

Helen jumped in. "Do you think, as a carpenter, that church building could support the weight of a big gathering of people?"

"Will it fall down around their ears?" Evangeline added.

"Well, no! That building looks awful, but it was around long before we came here, and I'm thinking it will be around long after we are gone. It's as solid as they come."

"Thank you, sir! We were sure hoping you'd say that!" the girls exclaimed as they headed back to Mr. Lauterette's office.

When his secretary showed the Duff girls back into his office the same afternoon they had just been there, he was amazed. "You girls back so soon? Did you forget to tell me something? Don't tell me you found two carpenters already."

Helen stepped forward. "Mr. Lauterette, we did indeed find two carpenters. They both knew the building and assured us that it is stable in its structure. They told us in no uncertain terms that it would be here long after we were gone and not to worry about putting a large group of people into it. They said it was solid. What we'd like now is your permission to use the church."

The lawyer leaned back into his chair and chuckled. "Tell me your name, young lady."

"I'm Helen Duff, sir, and these are my sisters, Evangeline and Olive."

"Duff, huh?" Mr. Lauterette said. "Would you be any relation to the Reverend Walter Duff?"

Helen looked at her sisters and laughed, "Yes! We're his daughters!"

Mr. Lauterette shook his head and ran his hand through his hair. "Had I known that, I might just as well have said yes in the first place. Walter Duff's girls…of course. Sure, then, go ahead and have your meetings!"

It was work to get permission, but more work awaited the girls now that they'd secured permission. Debris and filth had collected in that old church building for many years. It was a huge task to clean it out. One thing in the girls' favor however, was that they were attractive young ladies—with a couple redheads thrown in, to boot. Before long, word got around that the girls were hard at work fixing up the old church. Soon a work crew of several young men had collected to help them out! Down came the old stovepipe, and it was brushed out. The empty window frames were covered over with canvas. After much shoveling and scrubbing, the girls were able to hold their meetings.

These experiences became almost common as the girls continued to look for places to conduct meetings. In another town, they found a closed church and went in search of someone with the authority to allow them to open it for their meetings. They began to go door to door, looking for anyone who could give them permission to use the building. Across the street from the church they met a lady who told them, "I can't tell you that you can use the building, but if you get permission, I have a piano you could use. If you need one, of course. We'll move it over for you—it's just across the street. Shouldn't be any trouble."

The girls thanked her and continued to search for the person who could tell them "yea" or "nay" about using the closed church. "Seems a bit backward to get the piano before we have a building," Helen joked. "I'm sure that means we'll get permission to use it!"

Helen was right. Before they'd gone much farther, they found the people who had the authority to let them use the building, and they received the okay to use the old church. As an afterthought, Helen turned back on her way out the door and said, "By the way, the people across the street from the church said we could use their piano for our meetings."

A surprised look came over the man's face as he replied, "Oh, girls, didn't anyone think to tell you? This church is the kind that doesn't let any instruments into the sanctuary. I'm afraid you can't use a piano there."

Thinking quickly, Evangeline said, "Well, what about in the vestibule?"

The man paused and scratched his head. "I sure can't think of a reason why not. The rule only says the sanctuary is off limits."

By that evening, the girls had things all arranged, or rather, rearranged. They had tugged the pulpit to the back of the church and had the piano and their other instruments arranged near it in the vestibule. Then they had turned all the pews around to face the back of the church. The novelty of the new setup helped to make their meetings there all the more successful.

Another instance found the girls asking about using a closed church. Olive asked, "Where is the key to the church?"

A lady replied, "That's a good question! Let's see," she said as she turned to the man next to her. "Who had the last funeral? That family will still have the key."

One of Helen's favorite stories to tell of this time involved a church whose bell was in the front churchyard and not in the belfry. The girls had already gone from house to house inviting all to attend the services they would hold that night. They stood on the porch of the church waiting in anticipation for people to start to arrive. Then, an idea came to them as they glanced toward the large bell.

"That's a great thought," Olive said. Agreeing with her, Helen and Evangeline said, "Let's do it! We'll call the people to service by ringing the bell. It's probably been ages since church was announced by the bell!" The girls could all remember the bells at the city churches ringing out each Sunday. They could tell which church's bells were ringing just by the different sounds.

Laughing, the girls ran over to the church bell and carefully, so as not to get their dresses dirty, began to pull the bell rope. Back and forth went the bell on its frame. Again and again, they rang the bell. "We're going to have to back away soon or we'll all be deaf," joked Helen. She was sure that loud bell could be heard all over the little valley where the church sat.

Sure enough, it worked! They began to see cars in the distance coming quickly toward the church from all directions on the country roads. The dust they were kicking up was tremendous! The girls were so glad such a great number of people were responding to the invitation to come to church.

When the first car drove up, a man jumped out almost before he got his car stopped. "Where's the fire?" he called out to the girls. What the girls hadn't known was that the bell had been moved to the churchyard because, for years, it had been used to notify the neighbors in the area of a fire!

The girls were embarrassed, but Helen was not about to let the opportunity to reach as many people as possible pass by. When the man asked where the fire was, quick as can be, Helen replied, "In hell! Come on into the church and hear about it!"

That little church was standing room only that night, and each of the following nights the girls were there. In spite of telling the man he'd hear about the fires of hell, the girls really spent their time telling the folks how to get to heaven.

The girls' delightful Irish accents drew people to them. Folks began to refer to them affectionately as "those Irish girls." From that sweet beginning, the sisters became known as the Duff Sisters Gospel Trio. They had much to offer: collectively the girls played horns, bass, viol, piano, marimba and concert harp. They also presented the Word of God in such as way that kept people listening. In a short time, the girls were in demand all along the West Coast. After a while, the girls divided up the duties at their services. Evangeline led music, Olive directed youth activities, and Helen became their evangelist.

The girls had lots of success in calling on homes when they reached a new community. People responded well to their personal invitation to join them at their services. But they also felt advertising was important. They tried all kinds of things to attract people to the meetings.

One time, when Walter was with them, he noticed some red flares lying by the railroad tracks. At once he had an idea! He got in touch with the station agent and got him to donate two flares. Walter finagled a way to attach the flares to the sides of their car. Over the top of the car, they fixed a sign with the word, "HEAR THE DUFF SISTERS GOSPEL TRIO TONIGHT!" Down the street they went, the girls in the back playing their instruments, the flares going off on the sides of the car, the sign screaming its message and Walter driving, grinning from ear to ear. Their impromptu parade brought them a standing room only crowd.

Once, while holding services, the girls heard of a terrible accident that took place in a neighboring town. A traveling evangelist who was doing meetings in that town and the pastor who was hosting him had been out calling on homes to invite people to the meetings. The men had been driving the car common in that day, a Ford Model T.

The Model T had three foot pedals: one for forward, one for reverse, and one to stop. Many people got mixed up about which pedal they were pushing, especially if they had to make quick decisions in an emergency. While driving up a hill, that's what happened to the pastor who was driving. He accidentally pushed the wrong pedal and instantly the car went into reverse and shot backward over a hill and into a ditch. The Model T landed upside down in the ditch, trapping the two men in the process.

The girls felt the blow almost as much as the locals. Since they traveled full time holding evangelistic meetings, they understood how easily their places could be reversed. So the girls decided that they would take a trip over to the hospital to see these men. When the girls arrived, a representative from the planning committee for the other town's evangelistic meetings was there, too. The church was devastated. Not only was their pastor laid up, but so was the man who was supposed to hold the meetings! On the spot, the girls were asked to cover the meetings since they were finishing up "just the next town over." The timing seemed too perfect to be coincidental.

The meetings went so well! Many people came to know the Lord through the music and messages of the Duff Trio. After the last meeting, the head deacon and his wife approached the girls.

"Girls, we were wondering if you might join us at our home tonight. My wife here has baked a couple of her award-winning pies and we'd sure like to share them with you. We'd be honored to have you stay overnight with us, since it's already getting late."

The girls looked at each other to gauge how tired the others were. When each nodded, Evangeline said, "Oh, pie sounds absolutely wonderful! Thank you for asking!"

Olive added, "We'd appreciate spending the night, too. We are tired after all these back-to-back meetings. It would be so nice to know we don't have to move on till tomorrow. Thank you!"

"Then it's settled," the deacon responded.

"Honey," the deacon's wife said, "Why don't we just have the girls ride with us? It's so far out there, they might get lost in the dark. They could just leave their car here, and we'll just bring them back after we're done visiting."

The girls agreed to leave their car, and followed their hosts out to the side yard of the church where everyone parked their various vehicles. It was dark in the country! No lights could be seen anywhere around. The girls stumbled a bit as they made their way toward their transportation. It seemed strange to the girls how they had to enter the vehicle, but they couldn't figure out just what was different. Once they were inside, however, it became clear to them. They were being chauffeured inside a horse-drawn hearse! The girls had a good laugh as they figured they were probably the most lively occupants that vehicle had ever carried.

Their travels offered the young ladies many things to laugh about, and many situations that caused some tense moments for them. But their journeys also offered frequent non-traditional learning opportunities. They learned things in the rural and coastal areas they could not have learned in the city. They learned to identify types of cattle from the farmers they visited. Fishermen taught them the kinds of fish in their area and the best way to prepare them. Loggers taught them about the woods. In turn, the girls taught these fine people about the Lord they loved so much.

True to their upbringing, family was important to the Duff Trio. Often another family member would join the girls on a road trip—one of the brothers or even their mother, Mathilda. When Haldane was eleven, he joined them on a trip to California. He was on his school vacation and was thrilled to be going so far with his big sisters. At one of the services, he decided to sit by himself up in the church's balcony.

After the service, the girls packed up all their gear and went to the home where they were staying. When they were all settled in with a snack, Olive suddenly sat up in her chair and said, "Where's Haldane?"

Helen said, "Oh, my goodness—we left him at the church! I'd completely forgotten he was with us tonight!"

Exasperated with each other, but also a little scared that they had forgotten their younger brother, they rushed back to the church in their 1927 Chevy. When they were about half way, there was Haldane, walking toward them. "Hey!" yelled Haldane when he saw a car approaching him. "Stop!"

The girls pulled over to let Haldane into the car. "What happened to you?" he asked.

"We were about to ask the same of you!" Helen answered with a little fire.

"Well, I guess I fell asleep on a pew in the balcony..." Haldane said sheepishly.

"We were that entertaining, huh?" Helen quipped.

"Aw, I was tired. I'm sure you all were great! Boy, was I scared at first when I woke up, though. The whole place was dark and all the doors were locked. I was stuck!"

"Oh, Haldane! How did you ever get out of there?" asked Olive.

Haldane puffed up his chest. "It wasn't too hard. I felt my way through the church until I found a window. I just opened it and crawled on out. And yes," he said, looking at Helen, "I closed it again." He laughed. "I remembered which way we'd come to the church, so I started out walking to see if I could locate you all. I figured if I didn't find you after a while, I'd stop and ask for help at a house, even though it was late."

Evangeline teased, "You're so cute, someone would have helped you."

As Haldane blushed, Helen added, "Or else adopted him!"

"Ooo, Mother would have been mad at you then," Haldane laughed. Everyone joined him, relieved that he was safely with them again.

In those days no missionary society existed that could use their funds and influence to send out the Duff Trio. So, sure of their calling from the Lord, the girls went on their own. They depended on God to fill the need they had for gas, food, and lodging through the offerings they received at the meetings.

On their way back home from Eureka, California one night, Olive, doing her part as treasurer, was going through the offering to see what they had collected. A shriek came from the back seat.

"Someone put a check in the offering for five hundred dollars!" Olive exclaimed. In the 1930s, five hundred dollars was a small fortune. No one could believe that Olive could be right. Immediately Helen pulled the car over. Cars in those days did not come with interior lights as they now do. So, all of the girls jumped out of the car to look in the light of the headlamps to see if Olive's eyes had played a trick on her.

Sure enough, written in pencil, was a check for five hundred dollars. "Who wrote it?" Helen and Evangeline asked together.

"I'm not able to pronounce it, but it's spelled L-e-T-o-u-r-n-e-a-u," Olive answered.

Helen was firm. "We'll have to find them tomorrow and take it back to them. They must have put the decimal point in the wrong place! We'll give the check back to them so they can fix it."

It turned out that Mr. LeTourneau was in the area to build roads. After inquiring a bit, the girls were able to find where he and his wife were staying. They drove directly to the house. The girls explained to R.G. and Evelyn LeTourneau their theory about the misplaced decimal point.

"Not at all," exclaimed R.G. "We meant to give you girls every penny of that check."

Evelyn chimed in, "We so enjoyed your service last night that we wanted to express our gratitude in some tangible way."

The check allowed the Duff sisters to attend the Bible Institute of Los Angeles (later known as Biola University). That was just the beginning of a long friendship between the LeTourneaus and the Duffs.

While in one particular town, the girls learned of a famous preacher who was holding meetings. The pastor at the church who had brought the Duff Trio in very much wanted to hear this preacher. When visiting about it with him, they all decided that it would be worth the time to drive over to hear him. As soon as their meetings had come to an end, they all jumped into their car and drove. And drove. In those days, thirty-five miles per hour was top speed. It took them many hours to get to where this evangelist was speaking.

By the time they all arrived, the parking area outside the church was full, except for one space. They all laughed that God must surely have wanted them there, because He had saved a space just for them. They ran into the church only to discover the service was already underway. As the time ticked away, they joked to each other that this man must be famous because he sure gave people their money's worth. After hours on the hard pews, the small group decided they'd had enough, so they got up as discreetly as possible and exited the church. As they walked to their car, they laughed about the possibility of needing to extend their own meetings by a couple of hours to give more return to their audiences—when they realized their car was gone!

"What are we going to do?" Evangeline asked.

"All I know is I can't sit through any more of that service," Olive stated emphatically.

"Well, we'd noticed that our friends happened to be in the congregation. Let's go in and see if they can give us any help," answered Helen.

The girls slipped quietly back into the service and approached their friends. After quickly explaining their situation, all of them exited once again. Their friends called the police and then took the girls back to their house for the night. The pastor also had friends in the congregation, so he found his own way home, after praying with the girls that they would recover their car.

The friends who took the girls in had nine children of their own, so they were used to opening up their home. They didn't miss a beat in adding three more people to the equation. They gave the girls a cool drink and sat them in comfortable chairs.

"We'll be right back," they said. Soon they were back in the living room, carrying huge stacks of newspapers.

"What are those for?" asked Helen.

With a twinkle in his eye, her friend would only say, "Watch. You'll see."

The couple began crumpling up the newspaper into balls and tossing them onto the floor. Before long, the place began to look a terrible mess. Still their hosts would only smile, and kept at their work. After hundreds of sheets of newspaper had been balled and tossed to the floor, the husband and wife team began to gather them together in the center of the floor. They covered them with a large sheet and tucked it all around the paper balls. This was to be the girls' mattress! It was tricky how it all stayed together, but stay it did. The girls crawled into a comfortable bed and slept in peace.

Shortly after the girls were up the next morning, the police drove up with their car. They could not discover who had taken it the night before. The only clue left by the thief was a dainty, lacy woman's handkerchief that had been left on the seat.

After thanking their hosts for rescuing them, the girls drove off. The ride back home had never seemed so short. The handkerchief had captured their imaginations. All the way home the romantic young ladies weaved story after story of the young people who'd needed their car for a romantic rendezvous.

When their brother Walter traveled with them one time, the siblings were driving on old Highway 99 to their next meetings. As they approached Albany, Oregon, Walter reminded them that they all knew a teacher, Judy, who lived there. Everyone was ready to be out of the car for a stretch, so they thought they would stop and see her. Her whole family had always told them to stop any time and to just make themselves at home. It seemed like a perfect place for a rest stop.

The Duffs found the house without any wrong turns, but discovered no one at home. In those days no one locked their doors, so the young people let themselves in. Before the days of refrigerators, people literally had "ice boxes." A block of ice was placed inside a compartment lined with galvanized metal. Then the food was placed inside another compartment above the ice. This allowed the food to be cooled without freezing or becoming soggy as the ice melted. Walter, ever hungry, peeked inside the icebox to see what might be there to nibble on. To everyone's joy, he found a whole, large watermelon. It was a favorite of all the siblings. Sure that if their friend was home she would invite them to join her in the juicy treat, they carved into the melon.

The Duffs ate about half the melon and covered what remained and placed it back in the coolness of the icebox. "Thank you, Judy," Walter said to the air! "That hit the spot!"

"Look at the time," Helen exclaimed as she put the rinds in the compost bucket she'd located near the sink. "I'm afraid we can't wait any longer for Judy to get home." As soon as Olive was done wiping up the table, the family started off again. They had hoped to be able to stop by Judy's school and let her know they had been there, but time had gone by so quickly, they had to hurry on their way.

It was some time later before the Duffs heard the rest of the story. While at a conference together, Helen remembered she'd never had the chance to properly thank Judy for her (unknown) hospitality.

"Judy, I never did get you written with a real thank you for the scrumptious watermelon that time we dropped by your house and took a break," Helen said to Judy.

Judy looked thoroughly confused. "I gave you watermelon? At my house? When?"

"Well, I guess it's been about two years now. I'd forgotten all about it until I saw you," Helen explained.

A smile played at the corners of Judy's mouth, a chuckle built up, and then she burst into laughter as she figured out what Helen was talking about. "Helen, I guess you didn't know, but I haven't lived in that house for close to *three* years. I've sub-let the place."

Helen looked at Judy in horror as what she'd said began to sink in.

Judy continued, "This explains so much to me! I'd gotten a really strange phone call from my renters about two years ago. They said the creepiest thing had happened to them. Someone had come into their house while they were gone. They'd helped themselves to a watermelon they had in their icebox. Whoever it was, had eaten half of it and cleaned up after themselves—all the rinds and seeds were thrown away, dishes washed, table cleaned, careful as you please. Not one other thing in the whole house had been touched as far as they could tell." Judy was laughing so that tears were streaming from her eyes. "I can't wait to tell them who it was!"

Helen was mortified. "Judy, I am so sorry! We had no idea you weren't living there. Oh my. We just walked into a stranger's house and ate their watermelon!" Both women laughed until their sides hurt!

Throughout the early days of the Duff Sisters Gospel Trio, the girls held their meetings in villages and towns where there was no other spiritual leadership: communities whose church buildings were closed, or in schools when a town had no church building. The girls would stay for one or two weeks and offer the people in the area good quality music and the truth of the Gospel of Jesus Christ.

During one such meeting, a pastor from a city church in Montesano, Washington, came to hear the Duffs message. After the service, he spoke to the girls.

"Why do you only go to rural settings? You should not confine your ministry to only small places. You should be offering this ministry in our city churches, too. You could be holding citywide evangelistic meetings," he said.

The girls like the sound of a larger impact, so they agreed to include some city churches and citywide meetings into their schedule.

The girls frequently found themselves in California. In 1928 while in Roseville, they met a young pianist named Charles Huddleston. Charles came from a Christian family and was highly recommended to the Duffs. The girls were conducting services in a theatre, and they asked Charles to come and play a piece for them. He was every bit as good as they girls were led to believe. The trio asked him to join them on the road.

Charles added a great deal to the girls' services. His playing was inspirational. And the girls were thrilled to have help driving!

Before long, their schedule began to be filled with city services, and they could no longer fit in time to go to the rural churches. Even though they were sad to be away from the rural folk and their ministry there, they each had a feeling that God had orchestrated the switch to the cities—and that He had plans for the girls far beyond what they could then see.

Chapter 4

Falling in Love

"If the church doors are open, that's where you'll find Elwood Baugh!"

That's what his friends said to tease him. Yet Elwood Baugh felt he was doing all the right things. His family was churchgoing. Elwood and his four siblings were all sent to Sunday school. As Elwood began to grow up, he developed an interest in his minister's daughter. Immediately, he also developed a deep interest in church! He began to not only attend Sunday school, but Sunday morning service, Sunday evening service, Friday night youth meetings, and Wednesday night prayer meetings. Before long, Elwood joined the church.

When his family moved to Campbell, California, Elwood was used to being active at church. So it only made sense that he look for a church he could attend. He once again threw himself into church life—this time without a girlfriend to motivate him. While still a youth, Elwood was asked to become Sunday school superintendent. Later he was asked to serve on the church board and to become one of his county's youth leaders. Church became his life. Then came a very special Easter.

Elwood's church had called a new minister that year. In anticipation of the upcoming Easter season, Pastor Farr announced he would be holding services every evening of the week preceding Easter. The congregation was excited to participate.

That Easter week, the new pastor spoke each night about what the Bible said about that day's events in the week leading up to Jesus' crucifixion and resurrection. There was Palm Sunday and

Jesus' triumphant entry into Jerusalem. Early in the week came the message about Jesus cleansing the temple. Thursday covered the Last Supper, Jesus praying in Gethsemane, His arrest and mock trial before Herod. Friday was about Jesus' crucifixion, and Saturday addressed the anticipation of His resurrection. Elwood attended each night and was mesmerized by what he heard. He felt he was experiencing each episode with Jesus for the first time.

On Friday evening, Pastor Farr spoke to his congregation on the mystery of Jesus' mission—how He stepped out of eternity and into time all with the purpose of going to the cross. The penalty for the sins of all mankind was dealt with once and for all on the cross of Christ. The wrath of God had been satisfied, and Jesus declared His mission fulfilled. In Jesus' own words from the cross, "It is finished," forgiveness was granted to a world much in need of it. All creation looked toward the day when Jesus triumphed over death, the last obstacle. His pastor said this triumph proved Jesus to be who He claimed to be: God Himself.

Then Pastor Farr made a claim that Elwood had not heard before: each person must choose individually to receive the forgiveness bought for us by Jesus. If we so choose, that forgiveness builds a bridge between the individual and God, creating a relationship that cannot be broken.

Elwood was sure he'd never heard this message at church. Must he really *choose* to have a relationship with God? Elwood was deeply moved as the service closed and the congregation sang one last song. It was a familiar hymn to the people in Elwood's church, *Just As I Am*. As he joined in the singing, Elwood realized that he had never done the simple things in that song's lyric: believing the promise that Jesus' death was for him, choosing to come to God Himself. It hit him as hard as if someone had punched him in the stomach. "I've come to the church, but I've never come to Jesus!"

Normally after the pastor said a closing prayer, he would leave the altar area. But this night he stayed and prayed. The congregation dismissed themselves quietly, each one feeling the solemnity of the moment. Elwood could not move, but remained in his pew, his head down.

When Elwood was sure he was alone with the pastor, he made his way up to the front to talk with him. Clearing his throat, Elwood said, "Reverend Farr, I'm not a Christian."

The minister looked at Elwood as if he'd grown another head. "Our Sunday school superintendent not a Christian? One of our deacons and our county youth director is not a Christian? Thank God you found out in time!"

On that Good Friday evening, Elwood's new pastor led him in prayer as he surrendered his life to the One who made him. Elwood chose, for the first time, to allow Jesus' act on the cross to pay for *Elwood's* sin, and thus start his true, intimate, personal relationship with God.

Little did Elwood know how completely this decision was preparing him for the rest of his life.

Back on the road with the Duff Sisters Gospel Trio, one minister had taken it upon himself to counsel the girls as to their future.

"Helen, God has given you all such gifts! The ministry He has blessed you with does not come along every day. You girls must continue on with this ministry and never marry."

The sisters figured this was God's way to let them know they should be in no hurry to marry. They thought God was confirming to them that they would travel together for many years to come.

But even good advice can be skewed. God was about to show the Duff sisters that when He plans something, no amount of good advice will be able to explain it away. And as September

1928 rolled around, God was about to let them in on another of His plans.

Not too long after Charles Huddleston started to travel with the girls, they were invited to go to Campbell, California, to hold meetings. Helen and her sisters had taken their places on the platform, ready to begin their program. A young man entered the church a bit late, and his movement as he made his way to a seat caught Helen's attention.

"My, but he's fine-looking," Helen thought. And before she could reign in her thoughts, into her head popped the idea, "He looks like a man I'd like to marry." Helen was so surprised at herself. Here she was about to do ministry, and she was swooning over a man! But still, there was definitely something special about this young man.

The minister of the church invited the girls to his home after the service. And, to Helen's secret delight, he also invited the young man. Always famished after a service, the girls never turned down a chance for a bite to eat.

Getting to know the people at the minister's home, Helen learned that the name of the mystery man was Elwood Baugh and he worked at a large bank in San Jose. All three sisters immediately felt at home with Elwood. Helen particularly paid attention to him that evening.

She watched Elwood. He seemed quite relaxed and at home in the minister's house. Helen watched as he helped the minister's wife serve refreshments—and then he cleared the table and went to the kitchen to help with the dishes. After a couple of trips to the kitchen, Helen got up and followed Elwood, quickly grabbing some dirty dishes on her way out. Over the sudsy water, Helen and Elwood visited and laughed together.

The meetings in Campbell lasted three weeks. Since it was already Elwood's habit to be at church "whenever the doors were open," he and Helen found lots of time to spend together. He discovered her to be great fun, full of life, and always ready to laugh. She, in turn, found him to be a steady young man, with a great mind and quick wit. Over the course of those three weeks, their friendship easily deepened.

When the Campbell meetings ended, the girls drove to San Leandro, California, for their next series of meetings. They had agreed to a two-week engagement there. Every night before they started their program, the sisters prayed with the minister. During the first week, the minister came back to join them and mentioned that a young man he didn't know had taken a seat in the congregation. The girls paid no attention to this statement, until they took their places on the platform. There in a pew sat Elwood. He smiled at Helen every time he caught her eye that night.

"I hope I didn't distract you tonight," he said to her afterward.

"Well, no, I wasn't distracted," Helen replied. She was curious as to why he came to hear them when he'd just heard them every night for three weeks.

"Could we go somewhere for some ice cream?" Elwood asked Helen.

Helen was ready to head him off, and she quickly responded, "*We* would be glad to go with you." Poor Elwood found himself taking three girls out for ice cream, when he had meant to invite only one.

Elwood was also a fast learner. After a few days of Helen turning his invitations into family affairs, he said to her, "How would you like to take a ride up into the hills and take a look at the lights around the Bay?" Before Helen could open her mouth to reply, Elwood added, "And could we go by ourselves?"

What could she say? Helen agreed.

Up there on a hill overlooking the beautiful lights around San Francisco Bay, Elwood asked Helen to marry him.

"Helen, I realize that God has a calling on your life, and I would never want to interfere with that. I have never met anyone like you and I'd be honored if you'd allow me to provide you with a home and help you fulfill your ministry."

Helen could hardly believe what she was hearing. It had never occurred to her that God would allow her to marry and do ministry…that a man could exist that would encourage her to pursue a ministry and still want her as his wife. Here was Elwood, telling her to take any speaking engagements that she felt were from God, and that he would support her fully.

Helen said she would marry him—how could she refuse when every hesitation she'd ever felt was dealt with by his words to her? Her father had taught her that she needed to always be involved in some type of ministry. She wondered how her father would counsel her in this matter? This young man might not be in ministry himself, but he had assured her that he would always make it possible for her to be in whatever ministry God brought her way. That was good enough for Helen.

The one thing that did put a bit of a damper on this whirlwind relationship, however, was her schedule. Helen and the trio were booked solid for quite some time ahead. She and Elwood wrote to each other daily, and their love deepened through their honest correspondence.

Elwood and Helen tried to find a time when they could be married. All their ideas seemed to fall apart, again because of schedule. Finally they figured out a way. Helen had every night booked solid. But the ingenious couple went to the next county from where her meetings were and bought their marriage license. They invited the minister from the church where the trio was booked to come with them and perform the ceremony. By waiting until three minutes after midnight, it made it three days after they had bought the license, thus fulfilling the legal waiting period. The couple was married on January 23, 1929.

The next day Elwood had to return to San Jose and his job at the bank, and Helen and her sisters continued their meetings. The Duff Trio had several months booked ahead before Helen could think about settling down into married life.

When the bookings were finally fulfilled, Walter joined Evangeline and Olive and they changed their name to the Duff Irish Trio. Helen was released from her commitment to the trio. With a grateful heart and not a backward glance, Helen was free to move to San Jose as Mrs. Elwood Baugh.

Only a year after their wedding Olive married the trio's pianist, Charles Huddleston, on January 28, 1930. In 1936, also on January 28, Evangeline married Archie McNeill, son of the famous Scottish preacher John McNeill. Those wedding bells started new lives for the Duff sisters, and the trio was a thing of the past.

What followed were many years of happy family life. San Jose proved to be a lovely city to live in. Tree-lined streets and trim houses made Helen feel at home right away. When Helen arrived, Elwood was already established in the community. He had a solid job at a bank there. But, as for everyone, married life brought adjustments for the newlyweds.

Helen was used to a life full of movement and activity. She would get up in the morning, make breakfast for herself and Elwood, and then walk with Elwood to the bank. When she returned home, she found plenty to do to keep herself busy. Helen enjoyed being a homemaker, but was starved for conversation by the time Elwood came home at night. She always had a nice meal ready for him and he was very appreciative. After dinner, they would clean up the dishes and then sit in the living room together. Elwood enjoyed reading the paper, and Helen often sat by him reading a book.

One evening, however, Helen was not in a mood to read. She'd had enough quiet all day. She wanted to talk to Elwood—she didn't care about what!

Shutting her book and placing it on the table by the couch, Helen looked up at Elwood and said, somewhat pleadingly, "Elwood, talk to me."

Elwood looked at her earnest face, and put his paper down. He reached for her hand and held it between his two hands. "Helen, you know I love to talk to you. But I talk all day at the bank! It about wears me out. Could I just be quiet for a while? It makes me so happy to just sit here with you, even without conversation. I love just being with you."

Helen hadn't thought about him having to talk all day. He knew she didn't get to talk all day, but his answer satisfied her. She snuggled up against Elwood and they had an intimate, quiet evening being together. She was surprised that she could ever feel content just sitting next to someone and not saying anything! In their companionable silence, God confirmed to her, again, just how perfectly matched she and Elwood were.

Summers were spent outdoors as much as the couple was able. Elwood loved to fish, and so trips to Oregon to see Helen's family meant good fishing for Elwood.

Before too long, children came in to their lives. First came Eva May, and then Gordon. Helen loved being a mommie. She was fun loving and made a game out of many things that might be drudgery.

Discipline and training were, to her, a positive thing and so Helen took a positive approach to them. Instead of saying over and over again, "Don't do this, or don't do that," Helen tried to be positive. Both she and Elwood tried to find teachable moments and use those to bring insight and even adventure to their children.

Helen knew a walk to the store could be a good time to teach respect for other people's property. So she would say to her children as they walked, "The Baugh children never walk on other's people's lawns."

The children looked up at their mother with their big eyes and repeated, "The Baugh children never walk on other people's lawns, do they, Mother?"

When they got to the store, Helen would say to them, "The Baugh children never touch anything on the shelf." Her children would repeat it after her. Helen was so proud of her children, because they never did touch anything they weren't supposed to touch.

Helen remembered back to her own childhood and the things her parents had taught her. She understood, as did Elwood, how important it is to know God's Word. They made it a point to teach their children Bible verses, and were so pleased at how quickly their young children seemed to absorb the Word of God.

One Wednesday evening at church, their minister said, "Let's do something a bit different. Let's see if we can find a scripture verse for every letter in the alphabet. Who knows a verse for 'A'?"

Little Gordon, sitting so straight in his seat, spoke up before anyone else could. "All have sinned and come short of the glory of God."

"Well, done, Gordon!" the minister said. "Now who can find one for 'B'?'

Up shot Eva May's hand. After a nod from the minister, Eva May stood up and said in a clear voice, "Be ye kind to one another."

"Excellent, Eva May. Now, 'C'?" he said, looking out to the congregation.

Gordon was on his feet in an instant. "Christ died for our sins according to the scriptures," he declared.

The minister nodded his approval and asked for "D".

Again the Baugh children beat the others to the punch: "Draw nigh to God and he will draw nigh to you."

And the same for "E", with: "Except a man be born again, he cannot see the kingdom of God." This continued on for several more letters, until the minister said, "I think we know the Baugh children know a lot of verses, but perhaps we ought to hear from some other people now." Helen had to help her children learn a hard lesson on listening the rest of that night!

What a joy it was for Elwood and Helen to watch their children grow and learn. It was even fun for Helen to teach the children to take on little responsibilities, such as hanging up their clothes, or making their beds. Helen felt as if she was really part of something larger, as she taught her children to do things, just as her mother had taught her. She knew she was laying a foundation her children would build on the rest of their lives. It was hard to imagine her little ones one day being adults, but she knew it would surely happen. So she and Elwood tried to always watch for moments to teach new lessons and principles to the children.

One thing Helen and Elwood did not have to struggle through was the in-law issue. They loved each other's parents and had many happy times with each. Helen's father was still busy with his Bible-teaching ministry and often her mother was alone now that her children were grown.

One day Elwood suggested, "Why don't we bring your mother here to stay with us?" In their back yard was a small cottage that they fixed up as a cozy apartment. Helen's mother had her own place, and her father could come there between his meetings. It was a good place, and a happy time for the Duffs. But, it was also wonderful for Eva May and Gordon to have "Nana" so near. She was a wonderful grandma and loved to read to the children.

During these years of the Great Depression and Dust Bowl, the United States employed many people in the Civilian Conservation Corps, called the "CCC." The CCC used federal

Duff family in 1915

Duff Sisters Gospel Trio

Helen in 1929 - preaching pose (holding Bible)

Helen and Evangeline in front of old car converted as a camper – during early days of evangelistic meetings

Five Duff children as adults with parents

Elwood and Helen soon after their marriage

Helen, young Eva May, Gordon, and Elwood Baugh

Helen's sister, Evangeline and her husband, Archie, and daughter – they took Helen and the children in after Elwood's death

Group picture of early dinner meeting of Kansas City Christian Business and Professional Women

Three women Youth Home Missionaries with car and trailer in tow – 1944

Eva May Baugh and another Youth Home Missionary – summer 1944

Group picture of two Youth Home Missionaries with a large group of children – 1947

First permanent office in Ft. Wayne, Indiana

Helen and three staff members on steps of Ft. Wayne, Indiana house

Helen Duff Baugh and Mary Clark – 1950

Manor house in 1950's

Living Room of Manor – 1950's

Helen with Eva May and Gordon as
young adults – 1952

Annual Conference Banquet
1957 Grand Ballroom of Presidential Arms, Washington D.C.

Group of Stonecroft women kneeling in prayer – 1962

Helen visiting with teenagers in Salinas, California-1962

Helen, Mary, and Dr. Cho in Korea

Helen and others meeting Madame Chiang Kai-shek in Taipei

Helen and bricklayers in the scaffolding of Morningside - 1970

Portrait of Helen in 1970

Helen visiting with two women at a conference in Montana in 1973

Helen visiting a couple at a conference in Pennsylvania - 1975

Aerial view of Stonecroft

Helen, granddaughter Susan, and Eva May at Stonecroft's 50th anniversary in 1988

Women greeting Helen at 1995 conference

STONECROFT
MINISTRIES
WELCOMES YOU
WESTSIDE
SUNNYSIDE
CEDARCREST
INFORMATION
OFFICE
BAUGH CENTER
CHAPEL
MANOR

Manor

dollars to employ otherwise unemployed men to build public works projects such as bridges, parks, and dams. It was not uncommon on a Sunday for the Baugh family to drive to one of the CCC camps and minister to the men working on a project in the San Jose area. Elwood would preach and Helen often played for the men. Eva May and Gordon had to sit quietly while the service was going on, but they didn't mind because they knew what was coming next.

After returning to San Jose, the little family almost always went to Grandma and Grandpa Baugh's for Sunday dinner. The children so looked forward to this time because their grandparents took the Sunday paper. The children, after kissing Grandma and Grandpa, ran straight for the paper and pulled out the comics. On Sunday they were in color! While the parents visited about boring, grownup things, the children stretched out on the floor and read the "funnies." Sunday was a favorite day for everyone.

When Eva May was seven and in the second grade, she danced all the way to the car after school one afternoon. "Mommie, lookit! I got a report card!" she exclaimed with delight.

With great anticipation, Helen pulled the card from its little sleeve. To her dismay, the grades were not that good. *How could that be?* Helen wondered. Then she noticed that the teacher had made some comments in the box at the bottom. "Eva May finds it hard to concentrate. Perhaps you could help her at home," the note read.

That night after dinner, Helen handed the report card to Elwood. Before he opened it, she told him, "Your little girl is not doing too well."

Elwood raised his eyebrows and opened the report card. He quietly read the note from Eva May's teacher and then said, "Well, it's only because she hasn't learned how to concentrate yet. I'll help her and she'll do just fine."

A few days later, Helen reminded him to sign the report card so Eva May could take it back to school. He did, and Helen thought no more about it.

Another six weeks went by and it was report card time again. While she and Eva May waited in the car for Gordon, Helen pulled the card out, anxious to see if there had been any improvement since Elwood had been helping their daughter. Yes, the grades had come up! Helen checked to see if any new comments were there. The teacher had written, "Eva May is much improved."

Then Helen noticed her husband's handwriting. Curious, she read his note in the "parent's comments" portion from the previous term. "Sorry Eva May finds it hard to concentrate. She's just like her mother: I'm working on both of them. E.B. Baugh." Helen was not sure what to think! She decided that Elwood was playing with her, and that this term, it was her turn to write the comments.

When it came time to return the report card to school, Helen wrote, "So glad Eva May is improved. Soon she'll be as perfect as her daddy. Helen D. Baugh."

This tit-for-tat dialogue continued all school year. At the end of the year when Helen accompanied her children to their rooms to pick up their belongings for the summer, Eva May's teacher exclaimed to her, "Mrs. Baugh, I'm so glad to finally meet you. Your daughter's report card is so interesting! I'm afraid the card has become a bit of a celebrity. The little notes you and your husband write each term had all the other teachers asking, 'Is the card back yet? Bring it to the teachers' meeting as soon as it returns!' It has given the teachers something fun to look forward to all year long. Thank you for your humor!"

True to his word, Elwood did not stand in the way of Helen ministering as she felt God leading. Eva May started first grade in a whole different town than San Jose, as Helen had moved to Wonder, Oregon to take a short-term pastorate in a small church there. When the meetings were over and the church steady on its feet, Helen returned with the children to San Jose.

Situations like this happened numerous times. Some trips were short in duration; others were long. Elwood would always tell Helen, "Your mother and I can look after the children, so don't worry. Do what God has asked you to do."

Even Helen's children understood at an early age how important it was for their mother to be about God's work. One day while Helen was away, little Gordon was outside watching his neighbor work on his car. Trying to be sensitive to how the little fellow might be feeling, the neighbor asked him, "Does it make you feel bad that your mother goes away so much? You know, for all those speaking engagements?"

Gordon cocked his head to the side and looked right at the neighbor. In his clear young voice, he said, "Well, I guess if my mother didn't preach the Gospel, the rocks would cry out!" That was the last time the neighbor asked about that.

The years in San Jose were a shining time in the life of Helen and Elwood. But even as life had settled into a kind of routine, God was about to do a new thing.

Chapter 5

The Foundation of Prayer

It's one thing to see "God Answers Prayer" in a framed cross stitch on the wall. It's quite another to see God answer prayer in real time.

From Helen's earliest memories, prayer had been a vital part of her life. It was so much a part of her training that it was as natural to her as breathing. She could remember specific times as a child of being called in from playing for a time of family prayer. She had seen God heal her mother as a result of prayer. She had seen friends and acquaintances meet Jesus in response to prayer. She knew that God had provided many times, in many ways, in answer to her parents' fervent prayer.

Still, it wasn't until after Helen was married that she began to give prayer a real priority in her life. Many things changed during her time in San Jose as God chiseled Helen into a person of prayer.

One winter Sunday, Helen's parents were visiting them in San Jose. Her father came home from church and told her that he'd met the nicest young woman at the service. He'd invited her to come to meet Helen, and to pray with her. Helen was not too surprised at this, because her father was always following nudges from the Lord. Helen took it in stride. In a few days, at her door she found a woman who would soon be a wonderful friend and her first prayer partner.

Ora Lee Sample came with a smile and a great love for prayer. She told Helen, "Mr. Duff thought we'd enjoy praying together." As the women got to know each other, Helen grew to love Ora Lee's sense of humor and how much fun they had together. The women met each Friday and prayed that God would use them to lead many people in their city to Christ.

Helen learned so much from Ora Lee! Together they watched God answer countless prayers. God used this time in Helen's life to confirm to her the important place prayer needed to hold in her life.

Before God brought the next phase of His plan to light in Helen's life, He confirmed in her the organization she'd been taught. Helen already was one who liked things in their place. Each morning she would make sure the beds were made, dishes washed and put away. She'd plan out what she was going to fix for dinner that night, and prepare as much as she could do ahead.

Like most women, Helen had learned to be a multi-tasker. She had a routine that she'd learned from her mother. Monday was washday. Helen would get the clothes into her washer and then fix breakfast. After cleaning up breakfast, she struggled to run all the clothes through the wringer, then hung them on the line to dry. In between the line and bringing in the wash, she worked on preparations for dinner.

Tuesday was ironing day. Permanent press clothes had not yet been invented. Ironing took most of a day, as everything had to be ironed, including sheets!

Each day had its chores, and Helen felt good as she settled into a routine. It would not be long until she was extremely thankful for her routine. It was one of the things that made the way smooth as God opened the next door for Helen to walk through.

Early in her marriage, Helen would do her chores for the day, have dinner planned and then realize the rest of the day was before her. She wondered what to do with all her time.

One day while thinking about this problem of time, she read the Bible verse that says, "...I give myself unto prayer." Helen felt the Lord speak to her heart in response to her musings. The solution was very clear as God said, "Why not spend more time reading My Word and communicating with Me in prayer?"

Helen realized with a start that she'd never had time to make prayer much of a priority in her life before. The demands of her busy, and sometimes frantic schedule while on the road didn't allow for long periods of time spent in prayer. Helen determined to do just that.

She asked the Lord to awaken her at six every morning. Her desire was to spend the first hour of every day with Him. The first morning after this commitment, she opened her eyes to see her clock telling her it was six o'clock right on the nose! Instantly she was aware of the presence of God. He had indeed come to wake her and meet with her.

Helen grabbed her robe, pulled on her slippers, and slipped quietly into her living room. Each day from then on, she'd kneel by her couch and spend time with her Lord.

Her hour over, she then fixed breakfast for Elwood and herself. They ate before 7:30, and by 8:00 they were on their way, walking together to the bank. In those early days, Elwood was Director of Personnel. Helen loved those times, their chit-chat as they walked together. Funny how she'd so wanted Elwood to talk to her when he came home in the evenings, and God had provided a way for them to talk in the mornings instead. She received his first words of the day, not the leftovers at the end of the day. She thanked God for His sense of humor, and for giving her what she most desired: her husband's attention—both in words and companionship.

Even if Helen visited with several neighbors who happened to be out in their yards on the way home, she still had lots of time on her hands once her chores were done. So she began to spend more hours each day reading God's Word and praying.

One day a verse jumped from the pages of her Bible. It said, "For where two or three are gathered together in my name, there I am in the midst of them."

"What am I doing praying alone?' Helen thought. "I need to get others to pray with me."

Helen recalled a conversation she'd had recently when she'd been told about the city manager's wife having attended a Bible conference. Helen was sure Mrs. Goodwin wouldn't go to such a thing if she weren't a Christian, so Helen called her.

"Mrs. Goodwin, this is Helen Baugh. My husband Elwood works at the bank. I was wondering, if it's not too forward of me, if I might come to pay you a visit?"

Mrs. Goodwin was surprised by the phone call, but she did know Elwood, so she told Helen to come. Their meeting was just what Helen had hoped. Mrs. Goodwin was thrilled to meet a young woman interested in prayer and she was glad to commit to a time of prayer each Monday morning.

"And I insist, Helen," Mrs. Goodwin said, "you must let me host you here at my home. Do you mind if I invite some of my friends?"

By the time the next Monday rolled around, Mrs. Goodwin had gathered five of her friends who were all anxious to pray.

Helen always passed through an immigrant section of San Jose on her way home. One day while driving home from the Goodwin's, Helen remembered a woman she knew who lived in that part of town. On a lark, Helen stopped to see her. As they visited, Helen explained what she had just been doing.

"Would you like to have a prayer meeting in your home on Monday afternoons? I go right by here. It would be wonderful to pray with you!" Helen said.

In her wonderful Portuguese accent the woman answered, "Oh, yes! I invite my friends. We pray in Portuguese, and you pray in English. God hear in all languages!"

It just grew from there. Helen kept thinking of friends who might like to pray. Before long, she'd started twenty-four prayer groups all over San Jose. The women met each week and prayed that God would open up a way through which they could tell others about God's love for them.

While her children were still small, Helen took them with her to these prayer times. They learned to sit quietly and play, and as they got a bit older they would kneel with the women and pray. Eva May came to think that most of her early life was spent on her knees! Helen was so proud of her children as ladies would ask her, "How do you get your children to be so good and sit so quietly?"

Later, as the children started school, Helen determined that she would always be there when they got home. She made it a point to wait for them at school to pick them up, or else to be back home by 2:30. Helen loved those times with her children, as they'd tumble through the door, faces flushed with the news from their day. She knew it was important for her to be there to receive them and let them pour out their hearts, the good and the bad, to their mommie. The only times she missed it was if she was traveling. Then she knew her mother was there to greet her children—a woman already well-practiced in listening to children's news.

Elwood watched the prayer groups grow with great delight and amusement. "I knew you'd get something off the ground before too long," he told Helen. "I'm so proud of what God is doing though you! Why don't you come down to the bank and hold a prayer meeting with any employees who might want to join you on their lunch hour?"

From then on Helen spent three hours at the bank on Wednesdays, praying with anyone interested.

Once a month all the prayer groups met together at a large home nestled in foothills. Often there would be more than 100 women gathered. The women broke up into smaller groups and spread out into all the rooms of the home. This way each woman had the opportunity to pray aloud. Starting at nine in the morning, the women would pray until around two in the afternoon. Their hostess would give them good Swedish coffee and pastry before they all left.

Helen had no way of knowing that another pathway was about to open up to her. Prayer meetings in place, God had plans to use Elwood to open a new opportunity.

Walking in through the door one day after work, Elwood called out to Helen, "Honey, I have an assignment for you!" It was 1939 and Elwood had been promoted to a larger bank in downtown San Jose.

Helen laughed, "Okay, what is it this time?" By this time in their marriage, Helen was used to Elwood's assignments!

Elwood gave her a quick kiss and, loosening his tie, started in to tell her the details. "Remember that bookkeeper I told you about whose mother died last week?"

"Mmmm," murmured Helen. "How is she doing, poor thing?"

"This morning she came into my office and stood right in front of my desk and asked me, 'Mr. Baugh, where is my mother? Do you know what happens to people after they die? You're a religious man—does your religion tell you where people go when they die?'"

"Oh, Elwood, what an opportunity. What did you do?"

"Well, she hardly got the words out of her mouth, when she started to sob." Elwood ran his hands though his hair as he spoke. "I didn't think she was going to be able to stop! I got out my pocket Testament and read her some verses, but I'm not sure it was what she needed. This woman has real troubles, Helen. I don't know what to say to her. I wish you'd come to the bank tomorrow and talk with her. She told me neither she nor her mother had ever been to church."

"I'd be glad to come to the bank, but the poor girl might like to be somewhere else to really talk. How about we invite her to dinner instead? She's probably lonely without her mom at home; it might help her to have someone else to look at around a dinner table."

Elwood grinned at his wife in relief. "You're right, of course. That's a great idea!" Giving her another kiss, he headed out to do some weeding in the garden. When he came in, he'd had a new idea.

"Helen, this young lady at the bank is not the first one who's asked me questions about God. What would you say to inviting them as well?"

Helen was about to open her mouth to reply that she'd do it, but just how many would she need to cook for—when Elwood continued.

"I figured it would be best if we all just met at a restaurant. That way we could spend our time talking and answering their questions. We wouldn't have to think about cooking and filling glasses and cleaning up. We could focus on the young ladies. What do you think?" Helen said, "Are you crazy? What I think is that you're wonderful! I like to cook and all, but I'd much rather talk to the girls! And how often do they get to eat out? What a treat!"

Back in the 1930s people seldom were able to eat out. The country was in an economic depression. Very few people had money to spend in that way, and it was considered a very special thing to do. So, Elwood had no trouble talking the young ladies into joining Helen and him for dinner the next evening.

Ten young bookkeepers from the bank came and enjoyed a seventy-five-cent-a-plate dinner. Elwood and Helen had talked it over beforehand and, even though they could get a fine dinner for thirty-five cents, they wanted to make it a special night for the young women. They decided to treat them to the nicer dinner. And because Elwood was paying, he got to direct the conversation. He kept them on track talking about heaven and how a person gets there. Much of what Elwood said that night was new to the young ladies listening. He and Helen had a wonderful time taking turns answering questions and encouraging the girls.

The meal over, everyone began to get up to leave. Several of the girls gathered around Elwood and Helen. "Sir, could we do this again next week?" one of the girls asked. Another added, "We'd like to, but to not burdern you, we could all pay for our own, 'if that's okay." Helen and Elwood discussed this with the young ladies. They decided to meet again in two weeks.

Two weeks later, eighteen young women gathered to hear what the Baughs had to say about God. Once again, they asked to meet in two weeks so they could invite friends. And meet again they did. The numbers grew larger, and the desire among the girls in attendance was to continue to meet. But the group could no longer visit around one table comfortably. There were just too many of them!

Instead, Helen and Elwood began to invite outside speakers to come and talk to the whole group. Invariably, the speakers were so impressed with the model the Baughs had developed that they asked Helen to come to their cities and start similar gatherings. Helen always answered the same way: "I'm much too busy with my own family and twenty-four prayer groups, not mention all the things I do at church, to be able to do that for you. I'm sorry."

It became clear that the young ladies wanted their regular gathering to become something more permanent. So the Baughs helped them organize what had been loosely structured. Officers were selected to serve as chairman, treasurer, secretary, as well as three advisors and hostess and telephone chairmen. Others were chosen to represent the different city churches. They chose as their name Christian Business Women's Council (CBWC).

It was important to Helen and Elwood that the group have a project, and not have their sole reason for existence to be the gatherings. After praying about it, Helen felt strongly that the Lord wanted the group to fund a replacement for the work Helen had done in rural America. A young widow was asked to be the San Jose Council's first missionary. She willingly accepted.

God was laying the foundation for the answer He would ultimately bring to the petitions of Helen's twenty-four prayer groups regarding new ways to share their faith.

One summer day in 1941, Helen was at her desk in San Jose answering a stack of correspondence. Her goal was to be completely finished with all of her letters by the end of the afternoon. Helen was on a roll when, much to her dismay, the doorbell rang. She glanced out her bay window and saw a stranger standing on her porch. She decided not to answer and kept writing. "Perhaps," she thought, "if I keep real quiet, he won't know I'm here and he'll go away." How she wanted those letters off her list!

The bell rang again. Helen thought, *Oh no! I've left the front door open and only locked the screen door. It's obvious someone is home.* Reluctantly, she got up to see what the man was selling. Before she made it to the door, however, God reminded Helen of what she had prayed that morning. "Please bring someone across my path today so I can tell him about You, Lord," she had said.

Helen glanced at the plaque on her wall as she went to answer the door. "Only one life; 'twill soon be past. Only what's done for Christ will last," the plaque called out to her. The stranger at the door would have a perfect view of that plaque. "Alright, alright," Helen said to the Lord. "I hear You!"

"Good afternoon," Helen greeted the man.

"Ma'am." The man asked, "Do you have any knives or scissors you need sharpened? I'll do a fine job for you."

Helen did some quick thinking. What did she have that this man could sharpen? Ah-ha! "Do you sharpen lawn mower blades?"

He said he could do that, so Helen led him around the house to where Elwood kept his reel mower. As he set to work, Helen struck up a conversation with him. He looked tired, so Helen went in to get him a bite to eat.

With tray in hand, Helen came back out and kept that man talking! Bit by bit, the conversation turned to God. Startled, the man turned to look Helen in the eye.

"Lady," he said, "I rode the rails into your town this mornin'. I have to tell ya, I wasn't havin' too good a trip. That train clicked along and I looked up to heaven and I said—out loud, too, mind you—'Oh God, if there really is a God, have somebody talk to me about You today.'"

Helen was mesmerized by his story. She felt like she wasn't even breathing as he spoke.

"Now I been up and down Ninth Street and all this way along Tenth Street, and don't you know you are the first person who has said one word to me about God."

Helen could see in her mind's eye all "up and down" those two streets and all the Christian people who must have come in contact with this man. What were they thinking? Then Helen caught her breath—she had tried to get out of even answering her door, too! How close she had come to missing the opportunity to tell this man about the Lord!

Helen's mind was spinning, yet one idea caught her attention. "Would you be able to have dinner with us tonight? I'd like so much for you to meet my husband," Helen asked with a big smile.

The poor man was not prepared for this request. He couldn't remember the last time anyone had wanted him in their home. He finally accepted her invitation and went on his way, promising to be back at dinnertime.

Helen had so much fun getting ready for that dinner. She used her good dishes, her best goblets, and her silver service. As she set her table for five, she prayed, "Lord, I suppose I'm being a bit silly going to all this fuss for someone I don't even know. But I think You sent him here, so he must be pretty important to You. Please let this evening go the way You want it to go."

Helen pictured Elwood walking through the door and asking her, "Who's our company tonight, dear?" It seemed to Helen that more often than not, they had someone over to whom they were trying to minister. It was one of the things she loved about their life.

Not too long after Elwood arrived and Helen had explained to him about their dinner guest, the doorbell rang. When Helen answered it, it seemed to her that a completely different man had come to dinner. He was clean and well-dressed!

Over dinner, they learned that their guest was from Texas and was in the process of making his way home. When the meal was over, Helen excused herself and corralled her children in the back yard. Wanting to give Elwood some time to talk to their guest about the Lord, she had Eva May and Gordon help her water the flower beds. They watered the bushes and flowers, back and forth and back again until Helen could stand it no longer. She wanted to know what was going on in the house! She crept up to the window and when she peeked in, there were the two men kneeling by their chairs as the man gave his life to the Lord.

God had answered the man's prayer. He had also answered Helen's morning prayer.

Elwood and Helen reminded their new friend that they would continue to pray for him. He'd be going home to his family a new creation, and they wanted him to know he was not alone.

Helen handed the man a postcard that she had pre-addressed back to the Baugh's address.

"Please let us know how things go when you get home," Elwood said.

The man left and Elwood and Helen never saw him again. Helen later was so thankful that she had obeyed the Lord when He prompted her to open her door to the man. Because, at that moment, neither of the Baughs knew that Elwood would never get the chance to lead another person to the Lord.

Chapter 6

Loss and Peace

Helen's father convinced her to come to Portland to help establish a Christian Women's Council there. Reverend Duff must have heard God's voice on the matter. The Portland Council took off like gangbusters. After a year, the women contacted Helen to ask her to come for their first anniversary meeting. The women in Portland had planned a special event and were inviting many people. All they lacked was a speaker, and they thought Helen the perfect choice.

Helen wrote a nice letter back to them declining the invitation. Had it been a normal summer, her family would have been making a trip to Portland for their annual fishing vacation. However, this summer they decided to do things differently and made plans to go elsewhere. Based on these circumstances, Helen made the decision that it could not be God's will for her to speak at this event. She didn't ask God, or tell Elwood.

The ladies in Portland were a determined bunch. After a week Helen received another letter. It said the ladies had been praying and really believed she was supposed to be their speaker. Wouldn't she reconsider?

Helen answered this second letter, writing, "Our plans for the summer are to go to the Sierras, so it doesn't seem to be the Lord's will for me to head your way." She offered them the name of a man she knew would be in Portland around that time and suggested they contact him. Still, Helen did not offer this matter to the Lord.

On a Sunday afternoon in June 1941, Helen and her family headed to Grandma Baugh's house for their regular family dinner.

Helen heaved a big sigh during the drive, reached into her purse and pulled out a letter.

"Elwood, I need you to help me with this. This is the third letter I've gotten from the Portland Council asking me to be the speaker for their anniversary meeting—next weekend!"

"You're going to go, aren't you?" Elwood asked her.

His answer startled Helen. She had expected, or perhaps hoped, he'd discourage her from making that journey. *Why* she would think he might do that, Helen was not sure. There had not been one time since their wedding when he discouraged her from doing any ministry she'd been asked to do. He had certainly kept his promise he'd made to her before they were married.

"Actually, I've told them no twice. I told them our vacation plans are different this year and that it just won't work out. I offered them a suggestion of someone else they might get as a speaker. It didn't matter! They still are after *me* to speak."

Then Helen read him the third letter. "'We believe it is the Lord's will for you to be with us. Please send us two glossy prints of yourself for the two Portland newspapers.' Can you believe the audacity?"

"Well..." Elwood answered slowly, choosing his words carefully. "Just be sure that by not going you don't step out of the Lord's plan for you."

In her heart, Helen did not want to be out of the Lord's will. But it was 900 miles to Portland! She did not want to make that trip and leave her family. Sighing, she resigned herself to pray and find out if those Portland women were correct.

Monday morning God woke Helen at their usual time of six o'clock. Helen asked God what He wanted her to do. She made sure He knew she didn't want to go to Portland, but would go if He told her to do so.

While praying, Helen had a brainstorm. She had heard some missionaries at her church tell how they determined God's will by asking Him to send them the money for it. It was worth a try. Who would give a banker's wife money to travel, after all?

"God, if You want me in Portland, have someone give me the money I need to get there." That prayer seemed very safe to Helen.

Helen received no money by Wednesday. She was relieved. On Thursday she decided she'd better pack her suitcase just in case some money came. She would have to leave by Friday afternoon if God answered that prayer.

That night, observing her packed suitcase, Elwood said to his children, "It looks like your mother decided to go to Portland after all."

Helen said, "Oh no, I haven't. I asked God to do something very specific if He wanted me to go. So far, nothing. But if He does, I need to be ready."

Helen wouldn't tell Elwood what she'd asked God to do when he questioned her. She didn't want anyone to give her traveling money! She still did not want to go.

Elwood gently put his hands on Helen's shoulders. "Helen, you've never kept secrets form me. Please don't start now. Tell me what you asked the Lord to do."

Helen could never resist Elwood when he looked at her that way. She told him what she had prayed.

Eyebrows raised, Elwood said, "Honey, don't you have plenty of money in your checking account? I'd be glad to put some money in there to cover this. Just say the word!"

"This is exactly why I didn't tell you what I'd asked God to do. You are the one person I can't accept the money from—I asked God to do this outside of our finances." Helen was determined to make this as hard as possible for God to answer. She did not want to do this engagement.

Elwood shook his head. "Have it your way. I don't get it, honey, but have it your way."

Friday, her last day to wait, arrived with no money. Helen was starting to feel as if she might actually escape this trip. Helen had her regular prayer time, got Elwood off to work and the children into the yard to play. She turned away from the door but before she could sit down, the phone rang. It was Ora Lee, her prayer partner.

"Hey, I heard you were thinking of going to Portland. Are you going this weekend?" she asked Helen.

Ora Lee had prayed with her about the trip, but Helen had not told her what she'd asked God to do. "I don't have an answer yet," was all Helen said.

"Will you meet me at my work at noon? I've got to see you today, Helen," Ora Lee asked her.

Helen agreed and was waiting outside Ora Lee's place of employment promptly at noon. Ora Lee got into Helen's car and said, "Let's go find a cool, quiet place to sit. I have something I want to tell you."

Helen drove to the park and stopped the car under the shade of a huge tree.

Ora Lee looked at Helen a bit sadly, and Helen wondered what she was about to hear.

"Helen, I received some bad news this week. You know I've been saving money for my vacation for quite a while. I was so looking forward to going…." Ora Lee's voice trailed off as she looked out the window. She took a deep breath and continued. "Yesterday my boss came in and told us, 'No vacations for the duration of the war.'"

In 1941, much of the world was already deep in conflict. War loomed over the United States. The impending war had effects on the economy and everyday life of the West Coast long before those effects reached inland.

"Last night," Ora Lee went on, "God woke me in the middle of the night. He told me very clearly that I was to give you this money to go to Portland."

Helen's eyes filled with tears as Ora Lee handed her an envelope full of cash. With tears spilling down her cheeks, Helen managed to say, "Then I guess I'm going to Portland!"

Ora Lee needed to get back to work. After dropping her off, Helen walked across the street to see Elwood. He was just walking out the door for some lunch. "Hi, there, Mrs. Baugh," he said.

Helen smiled up at him and linked her arm through his. "Hello, Mr. Baugh!"

"So, did you get the money to go to Portland, Helen?" Elwood queried.

When Helen told him yes, he stopped in his tracks and spun her around to face him. "Honest, kid?" he asked, as Helen laughed her "Yes."

Over lunch, Helen filled in the details for Elwood. He told her, "You get on home and finish your packing. I'll be home soon to get you to the bus station."

Helen made arrangements for a neighbor to watch Gordon when Elwood couldn't be at home, and packed another bag so Eva May could go with her.

With the girls tucked safely onto the bus, the "men" turned to walk back to the car. "It will be great not to have all those girls around, won't it, Daddy?"

"Sure thing, Gordie. We're going to have fun," Elwood answered.

Helen could not hold back her tears. The dear sight of her boys walking together tugged at her heart. She was off on a trip she did not choose to make. She knew in her heart that the day of making her own decisions was over. God had made it clear to her that He wanted to "call her shots." He would be directing from now on.

The anniversary event in Portland went well. The Council there had four young women ready to go into rural America to minister as Youth Home Missionaries. They were paid $15 a month plus any love offerings they received from the churches they served. Evangeline had placed one of the teams and the Council asked Helen to stay a bit longer to train the other team and place them in a community. Helen agreed to stay.

The first thing Helen needed to do was to help the young women find a car. The Council offered to give $150 to buy a car. In those days, a brand new car cost $800. The amount the Council offered would buy a nice used car. The logical thing, and what people did, was to head down to "car row" to find a car. That is not what Helen did.

Fifteen prayer groups existed to support the Portland Council. Helen went to several of the groups and asked them to be in prayer about a car for the missionaries. With that in place, Helen and her father went to visit some closed churches to find a place to send the second team of young women.

Helen's mother said to her, "Aren't you going to go find a car for those young women? It's not going to do much good to place them somewhere if they can't get there."

Helen didn't look up from what she was doing. "No, Mother, I'm just going to pray and trust the Lord to bring the car He has for those young women to me."

"You're beginning to sound a bit fanatical, Helen," Mathilda replied.

Helen was hurt. She figured if anyone would understand about trusting God, it would be her mother. She kept her feelings to herself, but when her mother mentioned she needed something from the store, Helen quickly volunteered to go. That would give her some time to pray and get her feelings in check.

"Lord, am I a fanatic to try to trust You in this way?' Helen prayed as she walked. She could not get those words from her mother out of her head! Before she realized that she was doing it, she found herself humming the old hymn *'Tis So Sweet to Trust in Jesus.* The words became a prayer as she sang out her desire to rest on the promises of God. "I'm so glad I learned to trust Him…Oh for grace to trust Him more," the song said. The song lifted her heart, and became a particular comfort to her in the months to come.

That night, she put in a call to her brother Walter. He wasn't home, but his wife Edith said she'd let him know Helen had called. Instead of calling her back, he drove over to see her. He wanted to show her the new car he'd just purchased.

While she was looking his car over, he said to her, "Hey Helen, you don't happen to need a car for those missionaries, do you? I just sold my old one to a man and he wants to unload his. I asked him—why did I do that?—what he was going to do with his car. He said he'd sell it or give it away. I asked him how much he wanted for it and he's only looking to get forty or fifty dollars from it. Do you thing you might be interested in it?"

Of course Helen was interested. They hopped right into Walter's new car and went straight to look at this prospect.

The car looked good to Helen. Walter gave it "the once-over" and declared it sound enough to go ahead with the deal. Helen offered the man $45, and he accepted. Helen put another five dollars into the car for a paint job and a few little things it needed. The missionaries had their car, the Council got $100 back, and God delivered the car to the door just like Helen had asked.

The team named their new car "Peter" because it was not always the most reliable, given to its own "car temper." However, it served the young women for three years. Their frequent trips to the mechanic allowed the young women to witness to him. Eventually, the mechanic gave his life to the Lord. God used that car for much more than transportation.

By the time the young women were ready to sell "Peter," cars were hard to get because of the war. The young women tried to sell it for less, but the man who bought it insisted on paying the young women $300 for it. God used that car to do all kinds of miracles.

Helen delivered the missionaries to Oregon and got them settled into their new community. By the time she returned to Portland, Evangeline and Archie already had a third team ready for placement. Helen went with these young women as well, and again helped them settle into their new home. She took time to train them in calling on people, advertising their meetings, and other skills that would help them.

After several days, Helen returned to Portland to spend another day with her family before going home to San Jose and Elwood. Helen was excited to return home because Elwood had changed the dates for their vacation. Even though she'd taken this extended trip to Portland, they were still going to take a family vacation. God was good!

As soon as Helen reached Portland, her mother told her that she needed to return a phone call that had come from Seattle. Upon making the call, Helen learned some young women in Seattle wanted her to come there to help them establish their own Council while she was still in the area. The Seattle group had sent several women to observe the Portland Council and had come to the conclusion that Seattle needed the CBWC ministry. They begged Helen to come and help them.

Helen told them she really couldn't come at that time. She'd been gone long enough from her family and needed to get home. But, having learned her lesson, Helen did promise to pray about it and see if God would raise up someone to come help them.

That evening Helen remembered several other calls and letters she'd received over the last couple of years, asking her to help establish Councils up and down the coast of California. Helen had always told them no. Sitting in her chair that evening, Helen wondered if God didn't have someone ready to go from city to city and start Councils.

Helen was already too busy to take on anything else. She was just spread too thin. It was time to pray for God to find someone to replace her. Helen determined that she'd try to get an answer about this matter before she left Portland. She decided to spend the next day in prayer, asking her mother to look after Eva May for her during that time.

"Honey," Helen told her daughter the next morning, "I'm going to spend this whole day in prayer. I want God to find us someone to start more Councils. So listen to Grandma, be good for her, and please don't disturb me while I'm praying. If you need anything, Grandma will help you."

Helen did indeed spend the whole day reading her Bible and praying. She came up with a few names of people she felt were good candidates to lead this fledgling ministry. She cried out to the Lord to raise up a leader, His leader.

Around 4:30 in the afternoon, Helen was overwhelmed by a sense of peace. She took this to mean God had answered her prayer and had chosen the person He wanted. She felt released from her burden to pray. She joined her family for dinner, glad God had released her while the food was still hot! That night, her last night in Portland before Eva May and she would return to San Jose, her two brothers, her sister and brother-in-law were all there for the meal.

It was July 2, 1941. Back in San Jose, Gordon and Elwood were having a fine time. Although Helen's trip had been extended past what she'd first thought the length would be, the boys had no trouble fending for themselves. Elwood was a good father, and he enjoyed fixing little meals for himself and his son. Of course, they were also invited to eat at other people's homes, so Elwood was often let off the hook.

There were several branches on the tree in the back yard that concerned Elwood. It seemed that one good wind could easily make the branches come down on the house. Ever a good steward, Elwood knew he'd better take care of the situation before anything bad happened. So while the women of the house were away, Elwood and Gordon tackled the tree trimming.

Elwood tied ropes to the branches he was cutting to better control how they fell. One by one, he made calculated cuts and lowered pieces of branches to Gordon. His son would then drag them out of the way to be cut up later for firewood.

Gordon heard a noise behind him. He turned to find his father had fallen out of the tree and he was not moving. He didn't respond when Gordon called to him. Gordon ran to the front of the house, yelling as he went. "Help! Help me! My daddy's hurt! Somebody help!"

The neighbors immediately ran to the Baugh house to see what had happened. The adults quickly took charge. Someone hurried into the house to call an ambulance. Someone tried to find the information to contact Helen. Someone else picked up tools and ropes and cleaned up the yard.

The Andersons took Gordon across the street to their house and tried to take his mind off what had just happened. "Would you like to ride a bike, Gordie?" What a treat! Out he ran to ride in their big circle drive. Later, the Andersons brought him across the street and put him in his own bed, telling him, "It won't be long, Gordie. Your mom will be here soon. You just sleep and tomorrow will look better."

While Helen was visiting with her family that evening in Portland, a beam of light began moving jerkily on the front of the house. Most neighborhoods did not have street lights in those days, and the only way to read house numbers after dark was to carry a flashlight. Soon someone was knocking on the door.

Western Union was delivering a telegram for Helen Baugh. Helen sat near the lamp to read it, while everyone waited for her to tell them what it said.

Helen looked up at her family, barely able to hold the note in her hand. "Elwood has had an accident. At 5:30 today. He's been taken to the hospital," Helen said with a flat voice. She looked from one to the next and begged them with her eyes to tell her it was not true.

Commotion broke out in the house. Helen could not move. All around her was movement, but all she could do was sit and cry. Eva May came to her mother and said, "Don't cry, Mommie. Daddy's going to be okay. God wouldn't let Daddy die." Eva May patted her mother's arm and tried to reassure her. "Please don't cry anymore. Mommie, please!" But Helen didn't seem to be able to stop. She could not be consoled.

People were packing bags, making sandwiches, making phone calls. By 12:30 in the morning Helen and Eva May had been bustled off into Walter, Sr.'s car and were on their way to San Jose. None of them knew it at the time, but Elwood died about the same time they began their drive. During that long drive, Helen cried and prayed and tried to make some sense of the situation. So many thoughts went through her head.

This just couldn't be! God had given Helen peace at 4:30 that afternoon, and at 5:30 her husband had his accident. Before she ever got back to San Jose, she somehow knew her husband was gone. It seemed God had answered her prayer not by sending someone else to take over, but by taking her husband away and sending her instead.

Helen thought back to the Friday she left for Portland and her conversation with Ora Lee. Through Helen's mind went the picture of Ora Lee handing her the envelope of money. Suddenly Helen realized that Ora Lee had given her enough money to get to Portland, but not to get home! Helen remembered asking God for the money "to get to Portland." She hadn't asked about a return trip. To Helen, this was another indication of where God was leading.

When Helen arrived at the hospital, she was told that her husband had already passed away. Her father took her home. The house seemed so quiet. Somehow the very life seemed to have been sucked out of it.

The next few days were a blur to Helen. Arrangements had to be made. People had to be notified. A service had to be planned. Helen was so glad her family was with her. How could she ever get through this alone?

In a quiet moment, Helen glanced out the window. Across the road was her little Gordie at the Anderson's house. They had been so good to let him go over any time he needed to be away from the hubbub of his own house. There in the neighbor's courtyard at the top of their circular driveway, Gordie rode around and around in circles on a bike. There was no need at the moment to stop him.

Helen was pleased to see so many people at Elwood's funeral. She knew how she felt about Elwood, but it was a comfort to her that he was loved by so many. As an officer in a large downtown bank, Elwood was well known throughout San Jose. He had also been very active in various ministries and at church. He'd been invited to speak at numerous churches between San Jose and San Francisco. He'd helped her start the first dinner group that became Christian Business and Professional Women's Club. Helen counted no less than twelve ministers at his funeral service.

When she knelt by his casket to say goodbye, the organist was playing *'Tis So Sweet to Trust in Jesus.* Helen knew it was no coincidence. God was telling her she could trust Him, even in this. She and Elwood had spent more than twelve years as husband and wife, loving each other and enjoying their children, serving God in many ways. Now Helen understood she needed to give God her undivided attention…and she chose to do so. She accepted Elwood's death as the will of God. And she received His peace.

Evangeline and Archie came up to Helen after the funeral and wrapped their arms around her. "Helen, you and the children come to live with us," they said to her gently.

When Helen began to protest, they said, "Now, you know we've just moved into that big house and there's plenty of room for you. Our little Heather will love having Eva May and Gordie as playmates. Then, when you're ready, you'll know they are safe when you follow where the Lord takes you. You'll be free to go establish these groups."

Helen thought about what they said. It made sense to her. But she didn't trust that, alone, any longer. Helen wandered into the bedroom she'd shared with Elwood all those years. There on the bedside table was the devotional Elwood had been using. On the date of his death was the scripture, "When thou goest, thy way shall be opened up before thee step by step." What a comfort for Helen to think God had been talking to Elwood just as He'd been talking to her, preparing each of them for their futures. Helen knew God would be faithful to His promises.

Helen received one surprise during those few days before she left San Jose. In the pile of condolence cards was the little postcard from the man from Texas that Elwood had led to the Lord just days before. The card was to let Elwood and Helen know he had made it home safely.

So, within a week of Elwood's funeral, Helen had packed up her little family and moved them to Portland. It was hard for them to drive away from their cozy home knowing they would never return; knowing that Elwood was gone; knowing that life would never be as it was.

In Portland, Helen set about making a new "normal" for her children. She enrolled them in school. She went with them to church and got them active in Sunday school. She encouraged them to play with the children in the neighborhood, hoping that new, deep friendships would emerge.

While she was doing this for her children, she was also in contact with the women in Seattle, setting up a time to come help them launch a CBPWC. She made travel arrangements, and housing arrangements.

And she grieved.

When fall arrived and Eva May and Gordon started school in Portland, Helen began her travels. Helen deeply felt the loss of her husband. As she traveled and went into restaurants alone, she saw couples come in together. The wound in her heart would open again, and she was not able to hold back her tears. Once, while at a minister's home for dinner, the wreath placed on the table as a centerpiece by her hostess took her by surprise. Visions of the wreaths at Elwood's funeral flooded back into her mind. She tried to explain as she apologetically asked the hostess if it would be possible to remove it from the table. She just didn't think she could eat a bite with it there.

This pain of her loss of Elwood only compounded the pain she felt in leaving her children. It was one of the hardest things she ever did for the sake of ministry: separating from her children. They had been such a happy family! The first eight and ten years of the children's lives, they had been a part of a loving and secure family. Helen could remember so many happy times.

They knew each day when Daddy's bus would pull up to the stop. The children turned the rush to greet him into a race to see who could reach him first. Their love for each other, father to child and child to father, was obvious. Daddy would always take some time after work to go out and play with Eva May and Gordon, teasing and running around the back yard until Helen called them to dinner.

Once, Helen remembered, San Jose had a freak snowfall. Eva May ran out to the yard, twirling around, holding her hands out to catch whatever was falling from the sky. She watched each flake as it landed in her hands and then melted. Filled with delight, Eva May called out, "Look! Look! See, the cornflakes are coming down!"

Helen and Elwood made sure their dinnertime conversation included the children. They loved to tell Daddy and Mommie all the amazing things that had happened to them each day. They planned their family vacations, trips to Grandma Baugh's or visits to Oregon together around the dinner table. Helen and Elwood tried to be involved in every aspect of their children's young lives. If it was important to their children, they tried to make it important to them.

Then, without warning, Daddy was gone—and in a matter of days Helen's children were uprooted from the only home they had known and all their friends. They were transplanted to a different city, sent to a new school. And, because of the call Helen perceived, within a couple of months their mother was gone, too. Often throughout the years, Helen thought of what it had cost Eva May and Gordon for her ministry to come to be. Helen was always grateful for Evangeline and Archie stepping up to care for her children. But they still weren't Mommie and Daddy. Helen often wondered if her children missed her and their daddy as much as she missed them.

Shortly after Elwood's death, Helen found a promise in her Bible reading one day. In Isaiah 54:13 she read, "And all thy children shall be taught of the Lord; and great shall be the peace of thy children." This verse helped Helen to trust that her children were being covered by the Lord.

During the years in which Eva May and Gordon grew up, it was common practice for missionaries to send their children to a boarding school. It was seen as the proper way to care for children who might not be able to withstand the rigors of the mission field.

As did most of the people who knew her, Helen considered herself a missionary. She had no home but where God sent her, or those few precious days she could be back with her children. After a few years, Helen began to think boarding school might give her children more of what she wished *she* could give them.

Another factor Helen had to weigh was the fact that Evangeline and Archie were praying about starting a conference center. They were drawn to a property in Cannon Beach, Oregon. To take one thing off their minds, Helen believed then was the right time to make a move with her children.

So Helen enrolled Eva May in Prairie Bible Institute in Alberta, Canada. Eva May was 14 at the time. Gordon needed to wait one more year, so he split up the year staying half with Helen's parents, and half with her brother Walter and his wife, Edith. That year was a year of change for everyone, as Helen's father went to be with the Lord. Gordon was a great comfort to his "Nana," staying with her that winter because she hated to be alone. The next year, he joined Eva May at Prairie.

Both Eva May and Gordon enjoyed going to boarding school. Along with the fears of moving to a new place came the delicious feeling they had of being grown up and on their own.

Helen did her best to keep in touch with her children. She wrote them long, newsy letters each week. She always included a dollar for each child's spending money. She loved getting letters from her children, and saved most of them.

Her traveling schedule did not permit her to see her children as often as she'd have liked. But Helen did try to spend Christmases with her children, either at school or at Evangeline's home.

On one visit to Prairie, Helen was visiting with Gordon. He looked at her wistfully and said, "Mother, will we ever have a time again when we will all sit around the table as a family and talk… like we used to?"

Helen's heart ached to hear that honest question! Gordon had been praying, "Lord, let us be a family again." It took a few years, but God answered that prayer by giving him a wonderful wife and children of his own. Helen was able to join them around their table and be a part of God's answer to a boy's prayer.

As her children got older, Helen tried to allow them not to be her "little ones" any longer. On one Christmas visit, her children met her at the train with a group of their friends. True to her nature, Eva May ran to Helen and hugged and kissed her. When Helen looked at Gordon, she saw how much he had grown. He was no longer her little boy. So, Helen reached out her hand and shook Gordon's hand. She hoped he understood her gesture as her way of affirming that he was becoming a young man.

One day a letter came from Gordon that concerned Helen. She sat in a train station in Philadelphia and could not hold back her tears. Gordon had told how he was a part of a work detail collecting trash from all the faculty's homes. But that conjured up pictures of awful things in Helen's mind. She couldn't wait to see him and find out how he really was.

When she arrived for her next visit, Gordon told her how much he was enjoying his work detail. He gushed as he talked. It was the one job all the boys wished they had—and Gordon got it! He was allowed to go into all the faculty homes and empty their trash baskets. The best part was that the faculty so appreciated the boys serving them in this way, that they always had cookies for the boys. Gordon was thrilled with this perk.

Eva May wrote often to her mother to tell her all about the fun she was having at school. But she was very full of life, similar to her mother, and found it hard to be reined in by rules. The discipline for breaking rules at Prairie was memorizing Bible verses. At one point, Eva May told her mother she'd already memorized fifty-two verses that year!

Vacation times for the children were spent at Cannon Beach Conference Center, for wherever Uncle Archie and Aunt Evangeline were, was home. The children enjoyed spending all their breaks at Cannon Beach. Helen joined them as often as she could.

As strange as it might sound to a person with a 21st century mindset, Eva May and Gordon did not resent the ministry their mother gave her life to. They had seen their mother raised up to start a thriving ministry. They had watched God do through her what few men, let alone women, had done. They were well aware, as they grew, that women in those days just didn't lead ministries—that was a man's place. Few women were called to a public position as an evangelist. But God had obviously made the way for Helen Baugh to what few women had ever done, and to lay a foundation for the future of women in ministry. Helen was an evangelist and her children believed she was in God's will to pursue that calling.

Later in life Gordon reflected, "Mom had an exceptional gift for evangelism. Even as a child, I knew that she was truly called by

God as an evangelist. If we had to take a backseat to that, that was fine. She had a calling like Deborah in the Old Testament.

"I know things worked out the way God wanted, and anyone who thinks otherwise is out in left field."

Eva May told a friend once, "If my mother had to make the choice again, I would want her to do the exact same thing she did. I know it was God's will for her."

One letter that Helen cherished from Eva May said:

Dear Mom,

> *When God instructed children to 'Honor thy father and thy mother' He made it easy for me. You are so much loved and have earned my love and respect which I freely give. I'm very proud of you and feel very honored to have a mother like you. I only hope my children can feel somewhat the same toward me. I love you.*

Eva May

Helen never got over the impact of that letter. It meant the world to her that the very ones most affected by the wrenching decisions she had to make accepted them—and loved her. It confirmed to her again and again that God was bringing "beauty from ashes" in her life, and in the lives of her children.

Chapter 7

Rediscovering the Vision

Helen concluded her prayer time with a rather solemn, murmured "Amen." She raised herself from the small flowered rug where she'd knelt for the last half hour. As heartfelt as her prayer in the last few moments had been, she had found it difficult to focus.

Little wonder. The time since Elwood's death had been little but a blur. The family had gathered around her and the children with such wonderful grace and love. Father and Walter had immediately taken on roles as protectors. Archie and Evangeline had opened the invitation for Helen, Eva May, and Gordon to join them.

Yet Helen felt very alone these days. Elwood was gone. Her children would live with Evangeline and Archie while she carried on the work of the Christian Business Women's Council. She was still deep in the process of grieving on the one hand, and preparing to face the very demanding world of fundraising and organization building. Where was all this heading? What was it about?

At least she had these few weeks in Oregon to sort things out. She knew Eva May and Gordon were doing their best to encourage her. At the same time, Helen wondered if, having lost their father, they might not be well on the way to losing her too.

There was a quiet knock on the bedroom door. That would be Evangeline, who spoke from the other side of the door.

"Helen, dear, Father is joining us for breakfast today."

That meant Helen needed her wits about her. Father was anxious for Helen to begin traveling again. She thought back to the first time he had visited her in San Jose and spoken at the council dinner. Helen's father immediately saw the possibilities in the outreach, and said so the moment they all returned home from the event. "Helen, what a wonderful way to reach business and professional girls for Christ! I can see this ministry going into every city on our continent!"

She had done her level best to dissuade her father from that vision. "Father, I'm not sure women in other cities would have the same kind of interest as our ladies here in San Jose."

"Helen, do you remember when God asked Moses what Moses had in his hand? Moses responded, 'Just a rod.' But God used that rod to do miracles before Pharaoh and in the wilderness. Don't take this lightly, Helen. God can use this ministry all across our continent."

Her father had been right about the interest in Portland. He had been instrumental in getting a Portland Council started and the launch had been a success. In just a year since its beginning, the group numbered 200. Now, God seemed to be opening new places for ministry. But dealing with the loss of Elwood and thinking about how all that would unfold seemed pretty overwhelming.

Helen brushed imaginary wrinkles from her dress as she looked in the mirror one last time before opening the door to greet her sister.

"Good morning, Evangeline. Does the Reverend Duff seem to be well today?"

"Fit as a fiddle, it would seem."

"Are the children awake?"

"Not yet."

"It's Saturday. Can we let them sleep while we talk with Father? I'd like to serve them breakfast today, anyway. That is, if you don't mind."

Evangeline nodded and smiled. "Helen, I think they'd love that. I think you would, too."

They chatted softly was they walked down the stairway and into the kitchen, where breakfast, Archie and their father awaited.

Once grace was said, the Reverend Duff began the discussion. "Helen, the call of God is on your life. You are an evangelist. You have a special touch of God in sharing the Gospel with other women. God confirmed that call in you this summer."

Archie spoke quietly. "And it's so clear that Elwood was supporting you in this calling. Were he here today, he'd tell you to move ahead just as you are planning."

"You are a Moses of sorts, just as Father has told you." Evangeline reached for a plate of toast. "And we are here to help you as best we can."

"Welcoming the children and me into your home is a supreme help. I cannot ask for a better family." Helen looked at Archie, then Evangeline. "You think the children are settling in well here, don't you?" It was the only time there was any trace of anxiety in her voice, and then it was just a trace.

"I think so," Archie reassured her.

Evangeline nodded in agreement. "We'll all know better a few weeks into the school year. But I think they are adjusting very well, under the circumstances."

"In other words, Helen, you're free to do what you need to in order to spread these Christian Business Women's Councils all over the country." Reverend Duff brought the discussion to its point. "You can do the work of an evangelist, and train others to do the work with you as God wills it. But just as I did in Ireland with the Worker's Union, you have to turn your focus upon this enterprise as long as it is the means to fulfill God's calling on your life. If you do that, everything else will fall into place for you."

There was a moment of quiet before Helen replied. "I am still sad about Elwood. We had such a happy family life for almost thirteen years. But I had settled that I would submit to God and lead this ministry even before he was gone. And Archie, you're right: Elwood was encouraging me to move forward with the work of the Councils more each day. He will surely share in the reward of the souls we win through this ministry.

"I will need each and all of you to get this done, of course. Well, then. I'm off to Seattle when the children begin school. Let's see what the Lord does."

A few days later, Helen found herself in Seattle. She knew that, by most standards, starting anything of substance while the country was moving into another World War was a God-sized venture.

Those who knew Helen Duff Baugh understood God's unique gifting in her as an evangelist. If anyone had the opportunity to hear her speak, they were soon convinced that God had His hand on her in a special way. This multiplied her impact in at least two ways as more men went into the military to be deployed outside of the United States. First, more women than ever were engaged in business, making the expansion of the Christian Business Women's Council very timely. Second, people became more comfortable with women leading organizations and initiatives in the absence of men, making Helen's role as a leader far easier to accept in the American church and the culture than it might have been in an earlier time.

Still, there were a number of challenges that would have to be met. Everyday materials were being committed to the war effort, making them less available for civilian use. As the war continued and rationing became a way of life, finding items such as clothing, food, tires and office supplies to keep the ministry moving ahead would become issues of prayer—not simply due to budget constraints, but also because sometimes they weren't easily found.

Maybe Helen *was* more like Moses than she'd thought! Yet if that was the case, God brought her the help she needed to make it through the launch phase of the ministry.

Seattle was waiting for a Christian Business Women's Council. Still, Helen ventured into a situation where she knew no one, having come on the invitation of a stranger. Helen's hosts in Seattle, however, were a young businesswoman named Jean Scott and her mother. Jean was so kind and capable that she became the first chairman of the Seattle Council.

Helen knew no one in Spokane, either. So she headed for the Christian bookstore there to ask the names of businesswomen in the city. Enthusiasm to establish a Council grew quickly, and in six weeks Helen and some very sharp Christian businesswomen established the Spokane Council.

After a brief visit with Archie and Evangeline and the children, Evangeline suggested that Helen go to Vancouver, Washington, to start a Council there. She knew a young woman, Miriam Bracken, in that city who attended church where Archie was pastor.

Miriam was well-connected in Vancouver and delighted about the Council. When she learned that Helen was traveling alone, she offered to serve as her secretary and travel with her. If Helen was Moses, Miriam became her Joshua for a season.

Miriam was a graduate of the Bible Institute of Los Angeles and suggested that Los Angeles be the next city in which to establish a group. Because Miriam knew "the territory" of Los Angeles in general and the Institute community specifically, she was able to arrange speaking engagements for Helen to present the rural ministry at the Institute's chapel services. She also knew many, many Christian women in the city for contacts. Just as important, Miriam was an excellent secretary. The Los Angeles group was soon organized with Carol Kepple, the only female executive in a large department store in Los Angeles, serving as Chairman. Many of the women who served on that first Executive Committee were in executive positions in the business world. They carried on the Council in the same efficient way they did their businesses—more proof that God was providing more-than-able co-laborers for Helen.

For example, it took some savvy to plan events early in the Second World War. Members of the Los Angeles Executive Committee had to appear before the Rationing Board and were allotted a sufficient number of food stamps for the dinners. In securing speakers and musicians, the group had to keep in mind that gas was rationed, too!

In those days of gas rationing, Miriam persuaded Helen that train or bus travel would be more dependable than travel by car. They took the Greyhound bus when they left Los Angeles for Denver, a full-sized standard typewriter on their laps. (They couldn't leave it behind—typewriters were especially difficult for civilians to replace!)

Again, they arrived in the city knowing no one. So they networked. They heard about a meeting of the Gideon organization and decided to attend. The pianist for that meeting, Millie Stamm, and her husband Clarke became the local source of the contacts who would help launch the Denver Christian Business Women's Council, the seventh in the nation. God even led a local family, the Baers, not only to host Helen and Miriam but also to swap their portable typewriter for the standard model they would have carried on the bus to the next city.

God's leading and provision for the ministry were more evident wherever Helen and Miriam went. Yet Helen was reminded again that God cared for her personally while they were in Denver.

In the hotel where Helen and Miriam stayed before they met the Baers, Helen lost the diamond out of her engagement ring. As Helen later recounted, "We were just leaving for a meeting when I discovered it was missing. This was the only memento I had of my life with Elwood, and I felt really sad about losing it. We looked around the floor briefly but had to leave with just a word to our Heavenly Father who cares about every detail of our lives. When we returned to the hotel that night and turned on the light, my eye was caught by the reflection of something bright on the floor by the bed. Yes, there was my diamond, just waiting for me! We thought of how it could have been taken up in the sweeper or picked up by the maid, but God had preserved it for me."

The network expanded to include St. Paul, Minneapolis, and Kansas City. Then in Chicago Helen discovered that a "Christian Business Women's Council" already existed, so Helen changed the name of her group to the Christian Business and Professional Women of America. Miriam also arranged for Helen to speak in the chapel of Moody Bible Institute to recruit more young women for the Youth Home Missionaries program the Councils sponsored.

The Youth Home Missionaries program was birthed out of the Duff sisters' heart for the rural communities who had welcomed them while they were ministering as the Duff Sisters Gospel Trio. Even though Helen was busy traveling from city to city, her concern for rural people never left her.

Helen encouraged the Business Women's Councils to take on the support of one or more Youth Home Missionary. These young ladies, usually from the Bible colleges at which Helen would speak, would go in teams of two into rural areas of America. During the winters, the young women would hold released time classes for students from first grade through high school. In the summers, they would conduct daily Vacation Bible Schools. More often than not, they would also hold evening services for adults in their traveling ministry.

The initiative had a powerful impact in the communities where the young ladies served. As news of the missionary program's effectiveness spread, more Councils supported more Youth Home Missionaries. Forty-nine young women were providing vital support to rural churches through the Youth Home Missionaries program by December 1948, much to Helen's delight.

A Moody professor, Dr. Allan Fleece, encouraged Helen and Miriam to go from Chicago to Atlanta, Georgia where his mother lived. He was sure she could offer some good contacts in that city. God not only used Mrs. Fleece to provide the contacts that would help launch the Atlanta group, but also introduced Helen and Miriam to Pearl Abernathy, who in 1947 became the Christian Business and Professional Women of America's first National Prayer Chairman.

By 1945 Helen and the team God provided for her established eighteen Christian Business and Professional Women's Councils. By 1947, just six years after Elwood's death, there were twenty-six Councils in such cities as Atlanta, Chattanooga, Oakland, Omaha, Grand Rapids, Des Moines, Indianapolis, Pittsburgh and Dayton, in addition to those on the West Coast and in Denver.

Remember that no one had ever heard of this ministry when Helen and Miriam arrived in a city. As Helen later wrote, they "...arrived in cities where they were completely unknown to establish an organization which was completely unknown!... [Over time], many of these cities would have not only one Council but two as well as having one, two, three or as many as twelve Christian Women's Clubs! Nor could we ever have thought of these groups being established in cities around the world!"

Helen and Miriam established the first national office for the Councils in Fort Wayne, Indiana, in August 1946. Knowing that Miriam was an excellent secretary, Helen let her handle the office's coordination.

The organization had begun to hold National Council Meetings, week-long conferences usually held in August. During one such meeting, Helen was asked to go to Keswick, New Jersey to meet the director of the Keswick Conference Center. It just so happened that a couple who was at Helen's conference had planned to drive that way and offered to take Helen and Miriam with them.

When they arrived at the conference center, Helen noticed a young woman sitting on the center's porch. Helen didn't give it a second thought, but the young lady did. As Helen walked by, the young lady felt God revealing to her that she and Helen would be closely associated in some way.

The next day, Helen remained on the campgrounds to talk about her ministry at a conference when the rest of her party went on to New York. Glad for a break, she took a walk around the grounds before breakfast. She stopped in the bathroom to freshen up. There was that same young woman.

"I'm Helen Baugh," Helen introduced herself, holding out her hand.

"Mary Clark," the young lady responded.

Helen felt drawn to Mary from the start. Throughout the week of the conference, Helena and Mary spent long hours together walking and talking and getting to know one another. Both ladies had a passion to reach people with the Gospel. Helen shared about Youth Home Missions and the great work God was doing through it.

"It has been so exciting to watch God make a way for all these young women to serve Him. So little opportunity exists for women in ministry," Helen told her.

Mary was thrilled to hear of this. She might be able to direct young women with whom she worked into ministry through this avenue. Mary figured that this must be the connection God had spoken to her about. Mary later invited Helen to Maine, where her ministry had been based.

Mary Clark and Florence Wyeth, who had been a missionary to India, often ministered together and had led many young women to the Lord. Their doctor often called them when one of his patients was facing death and was fearful, lacking any kind of faith. Many of these people found a relationship with Jesus before death came.

Helen and Mary got to know each other. Helen was able to observe Mary at work, and was soon convinced that God wanted Mary to be a part of the expanding ministry He had entrusted to Helen. Mary's natural ability with finances and administration and her formal Biblical and theological training would be invaluable to helping to grow a solid ministry.

"Mary, please consider joining us in Fort Wayne. Our ministry could certainly use a young woman like you in leadership," Helen said.

Helen's request put Mary into quite a quandary. She had worked diligently to become a choice servant of God. She was greatly respected throughout New England. Could God really want her to give up all she had gained and move halfway across the country?

Mary decided that she would try what Gideon had done. She put a "fleece" out before the Lord: "God, if you want me to go to Fort Wayne to work with Helen, let someone place a check in my hand for one hundred dollars to be used for missions."

Mary told no one about her fleece. About three months later, some old friends dropped into see her. Mary told them about the new ministry opportunity she was considering. She enthusiastically told about the young women sent to do mission work in rural areas. Her friends instantly joined in her enthusiasm and made the decision to support a team of missionaries.

"Let's start this right now!" Reaching into his pocket, the man pulled out his checkbook and wrote out a check for one hundred dollars. He placed it into Mary's hand and said, "This is for missions." Exactly as she'd asked, God had given her a clear answer.

Mary got on the phone and called Helen. Helen had left the number where she could be reached in Philadelphia. When Mary called it, person-to-person, the operator said, "I know where Helen Baugh is tonight. I'll be glad to connect you." Of all the telephone operators in the city of Philadelphia, Mary happened on the only one who knew of Helen's whereabouts that night. Both ladies saw this as another indicator of God's leading.

In April 1948, Mary Clark arrived in Fort Wayne in her trusty Dodge. Mary became a great asset to Helen's ministry through her training in business and her natural ability in finances. Truly, she was the help Helen needed to continue in active ministry.

Still, it seemed always that finances were a common point of prayer.

The finances of the fledging ministry did not always keep up with the number of young women going out as missionaries. During one of these lean times Helen and Averil, a second secretary for the growing organization, were staying with the Deister family in Fort Wayne.

One morning as Helen knelt in prayer over ministry finances, she thought of the diamond ring Elwood had placed on her finger.

"God, could you really want me to give up the last connection I have to Elwood?" Helen cried out. "It would give us some fast cash…but it's so dear to me!"

As Helen prayed, she wiggled the ring from her finger. "I'll give it to You, Lord. You can use it to cover the money we need for the ministry."

Helen began to cry. Then she put the ring back on her finger.

"I can't do it, Lord!" Helen said through her tears. This episode was repeated a few more times as Helen offered her ring to God, and then took it back.

Helen heard a small knock at the door. There was no way to hide her teary face as her hostess slipped through the doorway. Mrs. Deister, alarmed to see Helen in such a state, asked, "Mrs. Baugh, what's the matter? Are you feeling alright?"

Helen got up to her feet and wearily said, "Yes, I'm okay." Mrs. Deister didn't feel that she could push the matter, so it dropped.

Helen prepared to leave the next day for a trip to Canada to visit Eva May and Gordon. As she stepped onto the train, she turned and pressed a small brown envelope into her secretary's hand. "Take care of this for me, won't you Averil?" Helen asked, and then turned and walked onto the train.

Back at the Deister's, Averil remembered the envelope and opened it to see what Helen had wanted her to do. Out fell Helen's diamond ring with the note, "Please take this to a jeweler and have it appraised. Then sell it and send the money to the office."

Averil began to cry because she knew the meaning of the ring in her hand. She knelt to ask the Lord for some wisdom. Again, Mrs. Deister entered the room as this was going on. Sure that she or her family had offended Helen or Averil in some way, she begged her to tell her why she was crying. Averil handed her the note, crying too hard to speak.

Mrs. Deister slowly read the note and then looked Averil in the eye. "Give me that note and the ring, and I'll take care of it for you." Averil was only too happy to not do that awful deed and gladly handed it all over to her.

A couple of weeks later, having visited her children, Helen was at her brother's home in Washington State when she heard a knock. With the day's mail, the postman had brought a small package from Mrs. Deister. "I must have left something at her house," Helen thought as she tore open the package.

There in the box lay her ring with a note. Mrs. Deister had indeed had the ring appraised. But instead of selling it, she had sent a check to Helen's office, taking the money from her own funds to cover the appraisal amount. Mrs. Deister assured Helen that God wanted her to have the ring Elwood had given her. Once again, God had provided the right people at the right time to strengthen Helen in her leadership journey.

That said, even leaders like Moses miss the people they love. Helen wore that ring till the day she died, another testimony to her of God's great love for her.

Chapter 8

Buying Property, Building People

There's a difference between someone asking you to work *for* them and someone asking you to work *with* them. Helen Baugh, it seems, always asked the latter. It's no wonder so many people were willing to come on board to work with her.

In the late 1940s, Christian Women's Clubs were added to the list of outreach ministries for which Helen and her team provided oversight. These noontime gatherings for homemakers followed the very successful pattern of the evening Christian and Professional Business Women's meetings. Because people were familiar with Helen and her CPBW team, launching a Christian Women's Club was far easier—especially in cities with existing Business Women's groups.

Of course, one challenge that comes with an organization's growth is finding the space to support that growth—and the space in Fort Wayne wasn't enough anymore.

Helen had never thought about the need to buy property for the ministry. She wasn't opposed to the idea; the thought simply hadn't entered her mind. Real estate, in many ways, was unfamiliar territory. Understandably, owning real estate felt like a big step. Helen and Miss Clark agreed to move ahead with two conditions in place: first, the money for the property would have to come through designated donations for that purpose. No general funds would be used for the property. Second, they would trust God for $10,000 by the end of the year (it was 1950) to buy property. Anything less than that would be God's leading that they were not to buy real estate at that time.

A prayer group in Atlanta heard a ministry representative tell about how the ministry was moving ahead and its need for a headquarters. In response, they gave $600 designated for the new property. Other gifts began to roll in from ministry meetings across the country. The books were about to close on December 1950 with a balance of $9,500 in the Headquarters Fund. The amount was nearly enough, but not enough. Helen took the amount raised as God's indication that they were not to move at that time.

But God wasn't finished. In the mail a few days later, a check designated for the Headquarters Fund dated December 28, 1950, came in the mail for the amount of $500. Helen wrote, "A note with the check told us that the donor had been awakened in the middle of the night and God had put it upon her heart to send us this gift from a fund that had been entrusted to her. When she had discussed this with her husband, he had agreed and so she sent the check. God had been faithful!"

The $10,000, all from gifts designated for Headquarters property, was in place. That began an earnest search for a property throughout the country. Mary Clark and Helen visited several cities in the eastern United States, hoping to find the "just right" property God had waiting for them. Coming with $10,000 in hand caught the attention of many real estate brokers along the way, but nothing the ladies saw seemed to be the right fit for the ministry.

Helen and Mary turned their attention west, where a speaking engagement for the Kansas City Council was scheduled. Verra Hughes and her family hosted the women during their stay. Because Verra was on the National Board, she knew her guests were on the search for headquarters property.

"Mrs. Baugh, I think Dad and I have found just the place for you right here in Kansas City."

Ever the practical one, Mary asked, "How much?"

"Oh, I don't want to tell you until you see it."

"Well, no use in looking until you tell us!"

Finally, Verra gave in. "$45,000."

"There's no way that we could buy such a place," Mary said, "so there's no use going to look at it."

Seeing the disappointment in Verra's eyes, Helen interrupted. "It doesn't cost anything to look at it, Mary. Let's just take a drive out to see it."

Mary agreed. Mr. Hughes reminded the ladies that this would be a country drive, ending about 17 miles from downtown Kansas City. About half an hour later, they drove up a small rise in the road and saw a beautiful estate on their left. A low stone wall surrounded the property. Tall stone pillars at the entrance held white wooden gates. A stately stone manor sat far back from the road amid tall trees. A big chain through the gates with a large padlock on it kept trespassers in check, and also kept the "search party" from going on the grounds that day.

Still, even knowing the price, they had seen enough to know that the property would likely be a great place for the ministry headquarters. They contacted the real estate company and made arrangements for a showing. Helen was quite taken with the property. She wrote, "As we passed through the lovely stone gateway and saw the pleasant drive winding up to the portico entrance, we thought of how wonderful it would be to use such a beautiful place for the glory of God. Situated in its lovely park, surrounded by spreading trees and rolling lawns, the stone house gave a sense of permanence and peace. Even in our wildest imaginings, we would never have pictured anything like this!

"Inside the 16-room house with its eight bathrooms, we moved from room to room, hardly daring to think that this could be the place God had chosen for us. Then we came to a small, beautifully-carpeted room tucked away by itself and we thought: 'A perfect place for a prayer room!'"

As much as they loved what they saw, the ladies held no illusions about the challenges they would face. Even though by now they had $20,000 of designated gifts in hand, the $45,000 price tag meant they'd need another $25,000. It just seemed like too much money. Even if they could raise those funds, there were no men in the ministry to care for the grounds. And being so far from downtown meant that cars would have to be available for the staff. They decided to forget it.

Helen and Mary continued the property search in other cities but, just as in the eastern United States, nothing they saw elsewhere seemed to be right for the ministry. After a few months, their thoughts turned again to the Kansas City property. The price hadn't changed. But this time, the ladies decided to try for a loan. One bank's policy prohibited it from lending money for property outside the city limits. A visit to a second bank produced the same response. Other banks and lenders seemed to have no help for them, either; and the owner had said it would be impossible for him to carry a loan.

So the ladies prayed. They asked God, if they were to have the property, that the owner would settle for $40,000 and that the loan to make up the difference between what they had in hand and the selling price be covered somehow. Then they had to leave to fulfill speaking engagements on the West Coast.

Verra called Helen while the ladies were speaking in Seattle. The property's owner wanted to talk to them, so they agreed to come back to Kansas City following their West Coast engagements. The owner, Mr. Kraus, had begun to feel strongly that their ministry should have the property; so strongly, in fact, that he was now willing to carry the mortgage. Mr. Kraus put the same information in writing and sent it to Helen and Mary in Seattle.

Once in Kansas City, the ladies met with Mr. Kraus and his wife. Mr. Kraus said again that the property was theirs if they wanted it, and that he would take the mortgage. It was then that Helen told him, "Mr. Kraus, we prayed very specifically about this property. We prayed that you would be willing to sell it for $40,000."

Mr. Kraus thought for a moment. "I can agree to that price with two acres less land."

Helen nodded. "We understand. However, we asked the Lord for you to be willing to give us exactly what you offered in the beginning, but for $40,000. If not, that's all right. We'll just know that the Lord doesn't want us to have it and He will provide another place."

"Hmmm. Ladies, I'll need to think about that. Please give me a little while to get back with you."

The ladies and the Krauses parted company at that time. It seemed that no one knew what to expect next. Helen and Mary were more than willing to return to Fort Wayne without a deal. The Krauses had already come a long way toward making an agreement.

As it ended, the Lord and Mr. Kraus weren't about to let the issue rest for long. Shortly after Helen and Mary arrived back at the Hughes' home, Mr. Kraus called. "Please contact your lawyer's office. I'm going to let you have the seven acres and house for $40,000."

Mary negotiated a contract in which the ministry agreed to pay $200 per month. She was also persuasive enough to have written into the contract the phrase, "or as much as we can pay." On May 27, 1952 the official papers were signed.

Within two days after Helen and Mary returned to Fort Wayne, they were headed back to Kansas City; this time with Lillian Baker and Elsie Widman. The four women made the manor ready for occupation. As soon as the new place was ready, which took just two or three days, they called Fort Wayne where Myrtle Baron was getting the furniture packed up. Two days later, the furniture arrived and the team began putting things in place.

It was July 1952. One of the first official acts at the new headquarters was to dedicate the property to the Lord who had clearly led them to, and provided for, the ministry's new home.

Carved into one of the stone pillars at the property's entrance was the word "Stonecroft." When the ladies inquired about this, they learned that the house had been built by a Scottish family named Abernathy. As is the custom of British families, they had named their estate. The word "croft" in the Scottish language means "home" so they named their stone home Stonecroft. It seemed a perfect fit for the manor and the grounds, so Helen decided to keep it. (As the ministry grew to encompass several corporations over time, its official name was changed to Stonecroft Ministries.)

The remaining donations needed to square away the mortgage came within fifteen months. Without any special fundraising campaign—only the mention that the ministry had bought the property and only gifts designated for the purchase would be used that way—the gifts began to arrive. Often a dollar, sometimes $1,000, the gifts added up quickly. The motto among the Stonecroft staff became, "Debt Free in '53."

By the time of the first payment, Mr. Krause had sold the mortgage to the bank that had first refused to loan money to Helen and Mary for the property. When the bookkeeper went to the bank to drop off the payment, she first wrote a check for the $200 monthly commitment. She handed a bank official that check then said, "We'd like to give you this, too." She placed an additional check for $2,000 in his hand—roughly the amount of designated gifts that had come in over and above the amount of the mortgage payment.

The bank didn't anticipate that the "or whatever we can pay" clause might mean that they'd receive several times more than the amount of the mortgage payment. But Mary Clark did. So the Stonecroft "mortgage payment *plus*" happened every month until the mortgage was retired in the third quarter of 1953. Even when bank officers came to encourage the ladies of Stonecroft to use the extra money to spruce up the grounds or buy something for the office, Helen and Mary were quick to respond, "We can't. We have to use the money for its designated purpose."

The mortgage burning ceremony was held in October 1953. "Debt Free in '53," indeed. The facilities for ministry headquarters were in place, and more than anyone might have imagined. Now the "people side" needed to be built up, too.

In a day when people expected ladies who wore pearls and sundresses to live life like Harriet Nelson or June Cleaver, Helen Baugh was certainly a breath of fresh air.

Helen truly believed that everyone who co-labored with her was, in his or her own way, just as important to the ministry as she was. To demonstrate that point, everyone on her ministry team received a subsistence salary—including herself. She wrote, "As part of the Stonecroft Ministries, everyone, including Miss Clark and me, receives a missionary salary which is far less than they could be earning in the business or professional world."

One thing that still astounds many who knew Helen was how quick she was to join in everyday tasks. More than one visitor to Stonecroft was welcomed into the Manor House only to find Mrs. Baugh washing dishes there. Helen's self-imposed tasks also included groundskeeping, laying bricks, sweeping, and mopping. One longstanding office worker remembered, "Mrs. Baugh walked by me one day and actually apologized for not being able to stop and help me file!"

This was a principle of Helen Baugh's ministry universe: Never ask anyone to do anything that you are not willing to do yourself.

That's why Helen was helping to rake and burn the leaves on the Stonecroft grounds on that fall day in 1952. That's why she reached across the fire and burned her arm. The fact that the Fall Area Conference itinerary began the next day kept her from seeking proper treatment of the burn. So that's why her arm was, by her own description, "really infected" by the time Helen's team reached the Pennsylvania Conference.

Eva Gilbert, a registered nurse at the conference, treated Helen's arm. Along the way, she pried the story behind the burn out of Helen. She didn't know what to think of it. Here was this completely classy, prim and proper lady before her who had lived with a severe burn on her arm for days without collapsing. Even more, Helen Baugh had been right out there working hard like an everyday laborer when she was injured.

Eva liked Helen's leadership style immediately. A head nurse at a major hospital in Harrisburg, Eva had worked for years in the Kentucky mountains as a nurse-on-horseback with the Frontier Nursing Association. She appreciated the value of hard work as did few others. As a certified midwife with a master's degree in public health, Eva also knew that the most effective training wasn't usually in the books but on the field. The more she talked to Helen Baugh, and the more she heard about Stonecroft, the more convinced Eva was that God calling her to take over the housekeeping service of the Manor.

Helen and Mary didn't believe Eva at first. They tried to persuade her to think over her decision to work at Stonecroft. But in the end, Eva won them over.

Without Helen knowing it, her example of leading by doing—without taking advantage of her position—had convinced Eva that serving God with Helen Baugh was a good thing to do.

Serving God with Helen Baugh had become a good thing to do for hundreds of women by the 1950s. From the beginning of the ministry that became Stonecroft, Helen worked to create positions in Christian service where women who shared her call to fulltime and/or public ministry would be welcome.

That desire fed the Youth Home Missionaries initiative, where female Bible college students and graduates could minister in rural areas through creative Christian education. It drove the appointment of the local chairs of Christian Business and

Professional Women chapters. It released the teaching skills of many women who were gifted in discipling others, and the organizational talent of others who would become national and international representatives for Stonecroft.

Story after story of Helen Baugh's recruiting methods reflect the power of personal contact. Helen's strategy was simple. She listened to the people God put in front of her. She encouraged them to take advantage of their skills and talents. Then, if God moved her to do so, she'd ask, "Is there any reason [or in other cases, "ten good reasons"] why you aren't in our ministry?"

In almost every case, Stonecroft staff who were recruited by Helen Baugh also agree that she made them feel like they were the only person in the room when she talked to them. Often, people talked with Helen about problems they were facing—losing a job, a broken engagement, feeling like God was calling them into ministry and having no place to go. Helen's ability to simply listen, take in what they were saying and then pray with them about their lives, changed the level of the encounter.

Jo, a Stonecroft ministry volunteer who first met Helen in the early 1950s, notes an important element of praying with Helen. "With Mrs. Baugh, it was never 'I'll pray for you,' but 'Honey, let's pray right now.' She followed through immediately."

Helen Baugh knew the secrets of building people, both as individuals and as teams. She led the way by example, starting with this simple principle: there is no task too humble when you are privileged to carry out God's vision in your generation.

As the Stonecroft staff grew in number and depth, so did the physical plant. Once again God moved mightily in bringing the remaining estate acreage to the ministry in 1954. With that added land, the ministry could build out to better meet the needs before it.

In 1955, construction began on a building that would hold eight efficiency apartments and an auditorium. The Missionary Center was the site for on-site Stonecroft training for many years.

In 1958, the Stonecroft Book Center was established to provide access to Christian books and resources to those involved with the rapidly growing ministry, equipping them with the truth of the Gospel, and the opportunity to grow as a disciple. As the staff grew, staff housing became a greater issue. The Stonecroft grounds eventually held six staff housing buildings.

The stables were gradually transformed into offices. The three-car garage housed the ministry's Multilith printing press. Modifications were made and buildings were added on an as-needed basis.

All in all, the Stonecroft property itself became a launching pad for ministries that embodied Helen Baugh's passion for evangelism—and the people she invested in that God used to make it all happen.

Chapter 9

Standing in the Gap

Their tattoos were nearly as thick as their biceps. They popped a dozen nickels into the jukebox. When the music wasn't loud enough, one of the bikers found a waitress and snarled as he pointed to the machine, "Hey! Turn this thing up or gimme my money back!"

The four bikers looked the part—black leather vests with huge gang insignias on the back, chains, and road grime in just the right places. Their very presence in the small diner made everyone else there uncomfortable.

Everyone, that is, except Helen Baugh. With a smile on her face, Helen walked directly to the booth where the road-weary motorcyclists had settled in. She smiled as she stopped beside them.

"Hello, gentlemen." Helen used a little extra Irish brogue in this encounter. "It looks like you've had quite a journey today. Are you from around these parts?"

At first, the bikers acted like Helen was from another planet. After a moment of stunned silence, one of them answered. Then another, and another.

"Tell me. I've never ridden a motorcycle before. What's it like?" The bikers had never expected anyone like Helen to express a genuine interest in their passion for motorcycles. They visibly relaxed, and in a few seconds were sharing what they enjoyed about their lives.

The conversation continued until the waitress came by to take their order. "It's been such a pleasure talking with you. I know you have a very good idea what a long journey feels like, and how good it feels to arrive at your destination. I want to make sure you arrive at the eternal destination God intends for you.

"I'm leaving you with these booklets so you can understand more about God and what He desires for you. You can choose where you end up for eternity, you know. No one but you can make that decision." Helen left a booklet that explained the Gospel simply and succinctly—one of the new LIFE booklets developed at Stonecroft for the express purpose of evangelism. Then she motioned to her team to come from the table where they'd just finished lunch to meet the bikers.

A few moments later, the Stonecroft team was back in the car headed to another speaking engagement. Mrs. Baugh looked around at her fellow passengers and said, "Now, we will pray for each one of those young men to make the right decision. Betty, you keep your eyes open since you're driving.

"Remember, we must keep an eye out for any unlikely people that we can bring to Jesus and do something about it when we can."

Any Stonecroft publication could be used for evangelism somehow. Yet Helen seemed to hold a special place in her heart for Stonecroft's LIFE booklets, which were specially developed for evangelism.

Helen remembered taking a train to visit Eva May and Gordon at their Canadian school. On the journey, a man walked down the aisle and asked if he might sit next to her. Helen said, "Certainly."

The man made polite conversation, asking Helen, "What is your profession?"

Helen replied, "I am a missionary to the United States."

"I didn't know the United States needed missionaries. What do you do as a missionary to the United States?"

"I tell people about God."

The man's voice took on a pleading tone. "Madam, will you tell me about God? I don't know about God and I would like to know."

Helen began explaining about God and how sin came into the world. Before long the train pulled into Calgary, where Helen would disembark for her visit with her children.

"You're not getting off here, are you?" the gentleman asked, looking startled. "Lady, you can't get off here. You are the first person who has ever told me anything about God, and you can't get off. No one I associate with knows anything about God."

The man was from Australia and was just completing a round-the-world tour. When he arrived in Vancouver, B.C. he would board the ship there and sail back to Australia. He begged Helen to stay over in Calgary one night so she could tell him about God. He said, "I'll get you a room in a hotel and I'll get one for myself in another hotel, and you can tell me about God."

"Sir, someone is meeting me to take me to a speaking engagement. But just as soon as I finish speaking, I'll sit down and write you a letter that will tell you exactly how to become a Christian."

"You'll forget. I'll never find anyone else to tell me about God."

Helen followed through, however, with a ten-page letter. She explained that the Bible says, "All have sinned and come short of the glory of God," but that Jesus Christ, God's Son, died to pay the penalty for that sin for each one of us. She explained how we must confess to God that we have sinned and must ask His forgiveness; then how we must invite Christ to come into our lives and live in us. She told him that in the Bible Jesus says, "Behold, I stand at the door, and knock: if any man hear my voice, and open the door, I will come in to him…"

Helen mailed that letter to the gentleman in Australia. Years later, she returned to Stonecroft one day and picked up a long, brown envelope with several air mail stickers folded over the edges. She looked at the postmark and noticed that it was from Australia, then opened the letter and read:

> *Dear Mrs. Baugh,*
>
> *I am the man you met on the train as you were traveling across Canada to Calgary. You began telling me about God, then you had to get off the train before you could finish. You promised to write to me, but I didn't think you ever would.*
>
> *Then one day a letter did come from you. In it you told me all about how to become a Christian. I read it several times, then slipped it into the top drawer of my desk at home. That was twelve years ago. Recently, my doctor informed me that I probably have only two weeks more to live.*
>
> *When I left the doctor's office, I came immediately to my desk, took out your letter and read it again. Then I knelt down by my desk and prayed the prayer that was in your letter. I invited Jesus Christ into my life. Now my sins are forgiven and I am a Christian like you.*
>
> *Don't bother writing to me, for by the time you get this letter it will be too late to write. But now I know I'll be in Heaven and I will be watching for you there.*

Helen did write to him immediately, but the letter was returned marked "deceased." It was that incident plus the thought of the hundreds of thousands of people all around her who did not know Christ in a personal way that prompted her in 1962 to prepare the first Stonecroft Life Series booklet, *Life Eternally Yours*—the one Helen handed to the bikers.

A series of booklets followed, each with a specific group in mind. Helen's longtime secretary, Helen Nichols, wrote many of these booklets, based on Helen Baugh's notes. Each booklet was written with the goal of seeing life and the world in the same way as someone might see it who had no relationship with Christ. What questions would they ask about Jesus? What would they want to know? What kind of story would really grab their attention?

Many thousands of people responded to the Life Series booklets who may have never taken the time for a conversation about the Gospel. In the same way, many Christians who wanted to share their faith but lacked the time for a number of face-to-face discussions used the Life Series booklets quite effectively.

For example, someone gave a *Life Eternally Yours* booklet to a tollbooth worker on the Kansas Turnpike. A letter from the worker's wife said that she and her husband had read the booklet and received Christ as a result. The letter also reported that their two college-age sons had become Christians, too.

An Ohio business man put copies of another Life Series booklet, *Would You Believe It?,* into each order that shipped from his factory. In one year, 800 people wrote to tell him they had received Christ through that booklet.

One afternoon Mary Clark and Helen were driving through Texas. They stopped for gas. Helen handed a booklet to the attendant as she paid the bill, saying, "This will tell you how you can know God."

"Lady, look in my station there," the attendant replied. "See that Bible open on my desk? As you drove up, I was reading my Bible trying to find God." Of all the service stations in that city, God had directed Helen and Mary to that very one.

Sometimes people found a Life Series booklet under their windshield wipers. Other times, the booklets came to them from a friend or acquaintance. Everyone from Little Leaguers to college professors to federal prisoners to fellow travelers are included in the number of those who have read a simple little booklet from Stonecroft and, as a result, received eternal life through Jesus Christ.

Helen Baugh wouldn't have had time to write a ten-page letter to everyone she hoped would hear the Gospel. For her and a vast number of others, the Life Series booklets are the next best thing—and maybe even more effective in reaching more people.

For years, there were no Bible studies held in connection with the Councils or Clubs that formed the basis of what would become Stonecroft Ministries. But by 1967, things needed to change.

In the United States, Bible teaching was falling out of favor. It was a time of cultural rebellion and moral confusion. There was no guarantee that any significant spiritual development was available to those coming to Councils or Clubs, even in the churches they attended. As Mary Clark and Helen Baugh compared notes from their travels across America, they determined that making sound Bible studies available through Stonecroft was a crucial step in encouraging inquirers to become believers, and believers to become disciples.

Lucille Sollenberger was chosen for the task. A Stanford-educated teacher and curriculum writer, Lucille brought a passion for God's Word and the ability to effectively introduce and explain it to others. Helen and Lucille bathed the project in prayer before Lucille put a word on paper, and kept it in prayer as it developed.

The studies had to be sensitive to the wide variety of people who associated with Stonecroft. They had to stay away from needless controversy and cut to the chase in the Scriptures. They had to embody sound doctrine without promoting the doctrine of a specific denomination. And, they had to be simple enough to be understood by the newcomer while being challenging enough to keep a serious Bible student interested.

The studies began with the book of Mark. This gospel account is a book of action, covering the brief ministry of Jesus Christ on earth. The possibilities of teaching that book according to Stonecroft standards excited Lucille. She began gathering materials, thinking through outlines, and praying specifically for God's leading.

There was also the matter of how to present the material in a way that would reach the uninformed and uncommitted. After much prayer and discussion, Helen and her team came up with the name *Friendship Bible Coffees*. It offered a non-threatening name around which to gather a group—and a non-threatening format to go with it. As Helen described them, "The Coffees would be held in the relaxed, informal atmosphere of a home where the neighbors would be invited to meet. Sitting around the table with a cup of coffee or tea, they would read and study the Bible together. The purpose would be to learn what the Bible really says and how to make practical application of Bible truths to our lives today."

Helen worked with Lucille to help her complete a prototype lesson. Lucille then returned to her ministry base in San Antonio to complete the study, which was completed and presented at Stonecroft's International Convention in August 1968. The next month the first 25 Coordinators came to Stonecroft to learn how to use the Bible Coffee studies in a friendship evangelism program.

Within 16 years, more than three million student books for the Bible Coffee studies had been sent out from Stonecroft. There were Friendship Bible Coffees in countries as diverse as Botswana, Malaysia, France, Germany, South Korea, Switzerland, Sweden, Brazil, Mexico, the United States, and many other countries. There were 18 different studies translated into 18 languages.

Yet the numbers meant very little to Helen Baugh unless she knew how they affected people in need of Jesus. This testimony was one of many that affirmed Stonecroft's decision to print Bible studies and present them through Friendship Bible Coffees. A Friendship Bible Coordinator from southern California wrote,

> *Walter Barnette was an extraordinary man: highly respected principal of one of San Diego's largest suburban high schools, tennis coach, outdoorsman, church founder, fine family man and community helper, and, one year after his retirement, elected as foreman of the Grand Jury! He was loved by everyone who knew him, but he didn't know Jesus Christ. His son did, and began to talk with his father about God and the Bible. Walt thought that he was good enough without all of that. Oh, he might have "struck out" a few times, but who hasn't? However, never being one to avoid a challenge, he began to look into this Book his son was so excited about.*
>
> *That's when he joined a couples' Friendship Bible Coffee. Walt and his wife and six other couples met every Tuesday night. Friendship Bible Coffees really made a hit with Walt when he learned what the Bible says about our relationship with God. We watched him turn into a wonderful man of God, a man who reveled in the Word of God as it revealed all that God is and had for him; a man who turned his whole life over to Jesus Christ when he invited Christ to come into his being.*
>
> *Several months ago, Walt found that he had terminal cancer and within seven weeks he was gone—gone to be with the Lord whom he had learned to love so dearly. His wife, Marion, and all who loved him miss him mightily, but we rejoice that he is with the Lord Jesus Christ forever—safely home.*

In response, Helen wrote, "How could we ever have known that God would use these lessons on such a scale to bring men, women, and young people to a saving knowledge of Christ; to mend broken marriages; to make Paul's prayer for the Colossians come true in thousands of lives today: '… that ye might be filled with the knowledge of His will … increasing in the knowledge of God.'"

People engaged in Friendship Bible Coffee studies don't miss their everyday value, either. One participant commented, "Friendship Bible Coffees have given me the necessary tools to convert faith and belief into behavior—they have bridged the gap between knowing and doing! I didn't realize the Bible was actually a recipe for living our lives on earth as well as giving us the key to salvation. I am so thankful to be learning and living the 'cannot-fail, success-every-time recipe.' It's practical!"

Late in life Helen Baugh wrote in her journal,

New days demand new METHODS, BUT…

The Word of God never changes.

The message of Christianity never changes.

The work of the Holy Spirit never changes.

Our commission to preach the Gospel never changes.

Bill Bright has said, "Several hundred million people would accept Christ if they knew who He was."

"I can't conceive of a person saying No to God, when it meant being born into a new family, having the peace of God and a home in Heaven."

For Helen in the 1960s, ministry became an issue of getting the Gospel to bikers as easily to housewives and school principals. It was a matter of making it difficult for people to say "No" to God by making God's Word easy to access and understand—especially in a time and a culture that had largely forgotten it.

For millions of people, Helen and her Stonecroft team succeeded wildly.

Chapter 10

Exploding the Impact

In the business world that has been surprisingly receptive to the ministries of Helen Baugh and Stonecroft, a company's brand is vital to its success.

What may surprise you is that a brand is not a logo, advertisement, or website. A brand is actually *what people think about a company or product when reminded of it.* Nothing more, nothing less.

A strong brand is one that is consistent, and consistently positive. A strong brand makes it easier to expand your product line. A new product from a company with a strong brand has a better chance to succeed in the marketplace, *if* that product reflects the values and standards of the brand.

One of the reasons Helen Baugh and Stonecroft Ministries were successful had to do with Helen Baugh's brand. Helen had three very consistent characteristics that made up her personal "brand":

» Her passion for evangelism. Helen had a genuine interest in people and their eternal destination. She consistently asked those who met her, "Do you know how to get to heaven?"

» Her dedication to prayer. One friend put it succinctly: "If you spent time with Mrs. Baugh, you prayed." Without a doubt, prayer was the foundation of Helen's daily activity and long-term planning.

» Her complete commitment to be a faithful disciple of Jesus Christ. Helen Baugh kept the Lord's work at the forefront of her life, and the lives of those around her, by asking, "What are you doing for God?"

The effectiveness of Helen Baugh's brand is that she passed on these three characteristics to the second and third generations of co-laborers at Stonecroft—not in a company manual, but in their hearts. The guiding principles around which Helen formed her life bore great fruit, and were demonstrated in the expressions of ministry in and around Stonecroft.

From the very first Christian Business Women's Council in San Jose, Helen encouraged the support of missionaries to rural America. Over time, Helen and her team organized the missionaries into a group called Youth Home Missionaries. These young women, usually students or graduates of Bible colleges, went out in teams to conduct evening services for the adults as well as afternoon classes for the children and the Daily Vacation Bible Schools. Pastors and church leaders wrote Helen to thank her for the young women's work ethic, dedication to prayer, and evangelistic work. Some of the Missionaries enjoyed long-term work on the field, which usually yielded even greater fruit for their time in a community.

In the late 1940s, the success of longer term Youth Home Missionary assignments were combined with requests from young couples who wanted to serve the Lord in rural America to launch a new work. Four couples were part of the first pastoral group of missionaries. Three of the couples were introduced to Helen by Mary Clark in Boston. The fourth couple had a more unusual invitation to join the pastoral group.

While Helen and Mary were en route to meet the couples for training at Cannon Beach in Oregon, they stopped to attend church near Minneapolis. During the service a young woman, child in arms, slipped into the seat next to the ladies and whispered, "Aren't you Mrs. Baugh? When are you going to start sending out couples to serve as pastors in the village churches as part of your project?"

On the spot, Helen and Mary invited the young woman and her husband to join the group for training in Oregon. It was clear to them that God was leading them to this new expression of ministry.

Yet they knew that they needed help in oversight of this new venture. Helen suggested that they drive to see her brother Walter, who was then pastor of a large and thriving congregation. If he agreed, Walter would direct a separate, self-sustaining organization for sending out couples. The couples would serve in a community as a resident pastor rather than being on an itinerary as the Youth Home Missionaries were. Helen and Mary would go on to Oregon and form a missionary society around the initiative, then prepare to train the couples at Cannon Beach.

Choosing her brother Walter to lead the new ministry was not an act of family favoritism on Helen's part. Instead, it was assurance that Helen's standards and worldview—her brand—would be extended into the new organization. Walter, having grown up in the same household as Helen, shared the principles that their father had instilled in them. He completely understood the need to share the Gospel. He was a man of prayer, and a student of the Word. He brought the Duff work ethic to the table, too.

Little wonder that Village Missions grew and thrived from that day forward. The organization placed hundreds of couples in locations throughout rural Canada and the United States, often providing the capacity to hold church services in communities where none had been held for years. Hundreds of adults and children came to know Christ annually through the work of Village Missions. Although Village Missions operated independently of Stonecroft from the time of its formal organization, the two ministries have always supported one another in prayer.

The initial focus of Christian Business Women's Councils had been on career women. When Helen began that ministry, most of those women were unmarried. When Christian Women's Clubs began with their focus on homemakers the question, "When are you going to have something for men?" became far more relevant.

Men accompanied their wives to the CWC conferences. The more they heard about Stonecroft, the more enthusiastic they became. These men were usually business and professional men, builders by nature, who were ready to impact their colleagues and neighbors with the Gospel. But they needed an avenue which would be inviting and challenging to these men. They would need something that would challenge them intellectually as well as spiritually.

They especially desired an opportunity that allowed them to be active. As various men learned something of the basic program and format of the dinners and luncheons, they became more and more convinced that this could be used very effectively for couples.

In response, Helen guided key leaders through the process of forming Couples' Clubs. Speakers chosen for these dinner meetings would include men from such diverse fields as a research physicist, a professional ball player, a rodeo clown, a dentist, and the vice president of an aircraft company. University professors and car dealers, accountants and salesmen, could all find these evenings stimulating and enjoyable.

As Couples' Clubs were established in various cities in the early 1960s, interest mounted. Couples were appointed to fill each position on the Steering Committee, and the men took the leadership role. The Clubs met from four to six times a year in especially attractive restaurants or country clubs. As was the case with women's Councils and Clubs, as well as the Friendship Bible Coffees, the Couples' Clubs endeavored to create a relaxed atmosphere so couples could easily get acquainted.

This method of outreach not only carried Helen Baugh's personal brand, it also affirmed the brand of evangelism pioneered by Christian Business and Professional Women's Councils and Christian Women's Clubs. The setting of Couples' Clubs was often on "neutral" grounds—a restaurant or country club as contrasted to a church. The surroundings were intentionally structured to be comfortable to those not familiar with the faith. For example, ashtrays were available for smokers. In restaurants where alcohol was served, guests were welcome to bring their drinks from the bar to the dinner table. Controversial issues were avoided in discussion and in special presentations. These nonjudgmental standards formed part of the brand that was especially effective in opening doors to share the Gospel with guests.

Men by the thousands have also been active participants in Friendship Bible Coffees. They respond well to the intriguing questions and solid Bible teaching in the curriculum, as well as to the fellowship in what often becomes a closely knit study group.

Even though the focus of the ministry was initially on women, God gave Helen Baugh and Stonecroft a brand that would reach men as well.

"Well, you've come at last! We have been praying for this day for a long time!"

This was the comment of a well-known Canadian pastor in 1966 as Stonecroft representatives arrived in Toronto, Ontario to establish a Christian Business and Professional Women's Council and a Christian Women's Club—the very first in all of Canada. The Canadian work grew rapidly under the direction of Canadian leaders who loved the method and the evangelistic impact of Stonecroft.

In her usual fashion, Mary Clark took care of the business and legal side of international expansion. The process she went through to establish bank accounts and file as a Canadian organization gave her vital experience as she guided the establishment of Stonecroft expressions of ministry in other countries.

Korea was one such country. Helen loved exploring other cultures, and the welcome she received in Korea only made her love it more. She relished the Korean hospitality. She loved the food. Seamstresses sewed native Korean dresses for every woman in the party of 162 that traveled with Mrs. Baugh.

Even more important was the reception given to Stonecroft's Christian Women's Clubs. Dr. Paul Yonggi Cho and his wife Dr. Okja Choi Cho, leaders of what would become the world's largest local church, pioneered the effort to launch CWC in Korea. Mrs. Cho became the first Chairman of the Seoul Christian Women's Club. Soon, an International Club and a CWC in Suwon also joined the ranks.

Shared values was an important consideration in the decision to spread the work into another country. Mrs. Baugh had enjoyed decades of affirmation that colleagues in Canada understood the mission and intent of Stonecroft. In Korea, she was delighted to discover the shared value of prayer. She noted, "One of the reasons Korea was so special to us is because they believe in and know how to pray! How well we remember that early morning walk we took to a local church where, at 5:30 in the morning, we found a group of people already praying fervently for their country. Then we learned that these prayer meetings are held 365 days of the year!"

Genevieve Ariege was born in Tahiti while her parents were French missionaries there. Later she moved to the United States with her family. In 1972, Genevieve was living in Colorado Springs where she was a secretary in a college. Despite the presence of a Council and several Clubs in that city, Genevieve knew nothing about them.

At that time, Helen was looking for a well-qualified person who could establish Stonecroft Ministries in Europe.

That Christmas Genevieve received a card from a friend in Paris, France, with a postscript that said, "You should come over and help us get CWCs started here."

Genevieve wrote back immediately to ask, "What is CWC?"

Her friend's reply included Stonecroft's address in Kansas City. When Genevieve wrote to ask more about CWC, Helen invited her to Stonecroft for a visit—and soon convinced her that God and Stonecroft could use her in Europe.

Before long, Genevieve was on her way to France to become the National Missionary Representative for Europe. In this capacity she started Christian Women's Clubs in France, Germany, Switzerland, Belgium, Italy and Denmark, as well as Friendship Bible Coffees.

That same year Eileen Genheimer heard about Stonecroft Ministries and thought of the wonderful avenue of outreach they would be in South Africa where she and her husband Don served as missionaries. Later, with the full consent of her mission board, Eileen was granted a year's leave of absence to work in establishing Councils and Clubs in South African cities. Soon there were more than 40 Councils and Clubs in four South African provinces, along with hundreds of Friendship Bible Coffees.

After serving as the Chairman of the Christian Business and Professional Women's Council in Kalamazoo, Michigan, Mary Barthold and her husband, Stanley, went to serve the Lord in Japan. In Osaka they established what became the largest Christian Women's Club in the world with as many as 1,400 ladies in attendance. Nearly twenty other Clubs became operational, along with scores of Friendship Bible Coffees.

Where she could, Helen made personal visits to help establish Stonecroft's presence in international locations new to the ministry. Whether she could travel to an international destination or not, Helen always made it a point to pray daily for Stonecroft's international workers and their ministries.

Over time, Christian Women's Clubs convened in Amman, Jordan; Jakarta, Indonesia; Bangkok, Thailand; Monrovia, Liberia; Port-au-Prince, Haiti, as well as in Austria, Belgium, Brazil, Costa Rica, Denmark, France, Germany, Greece, Ireland, Italy, Peru, the Philippines and even on the Island of Guam. The international initiative eventually took a number of Stonecroft ministry expressions to 60 countries around the world—quite an expansion from the first Christian Business and Professional Women's Council in San Jose.

How do the threads of various expressions of Stonecroft Ministries and Village Missions demonstrate the overall standards and values—the brand—of Helen Baugh and Stonecroft? Some years ago a letter arrived at the Stonecroft headquarters. As Helen told the story,

> *The writer, as a small child, lived in a mining town in Montana where there was no pastor. Two Youth Home Missionaries came to hold Daily Vacation Bible School and it was there this little girl invited Jesus Christ into her life. Later a Village Missionary pastor came to her community and through his ministry she was encouraged in her Christian growth. Because of Village Missions, she had a church in which to be married and a resident pastor to perform the ceremony.*
>
> *The influence goes on. Her sister married and moved to another state to a community without a pastor. She immediately wrote to Village Missions and a pastor was supplied. Through that Village Missionary, the sister's husband received Christ. The writer's brother-in-law and his wife invited the Savior into their lives through Friendship Bible Coffees and both became Guides. Her mother-in-law and father-in-law became Christians at a Christian Women's Club*

Guest Night. Their daughter began attending Club and she, too, became a Christian!

The writer's father was the most difficult member of their family to reach. Much prayer had gone up for him from his family. How good it is to know that God is personally interested in each of us. Through His graciousness, the Village Missionary pastor chosen to serve in that community had been a rancher just like this father, so they related well to one another. Shortly before the father went into eternity, the Village Missionary pastor introduced him to Christ. Nine members of that one family made reservations for Heaven through some phase of this holy ministry! And who knows how many other lives have been and will be reached for Christ through them!

Helen Baugh's standards and values fused into the character of the ministries God helped her launch. They were consistent, and consistently positive—especially for the people whose eternal future was changed by their impact.

"How often I have thought of the influence of one life on thousands of others!"

Helen Baugh thought of her father when she wrote or spoke those words. She would cite her father's life as a tremendous example. Helen would speak of her father leaving the family fortune behind to press forward and serve the Lord. She would talk about his complete and utter devotion to the Lord, and the influence God gave him both in Ireland and in the United States.

Helen especially emphasized the senior Walter Duff's influence on his own family. There is no question of Reverend Duff's impact on his children, either. Helen wrote:

Through Father's life and dedication, as well as that of my godly mother, all five of their children chose to enter the service of the Lord. In our early years, we three girls were busy opening closed churches and traveling as a trio, first in the villages and then in the cities of our land. Both of my brothers, Walter and Haldane, held evangelistic meetings, and Haldane had a Bible quiz radio program.

Although I did not marry a minister, God used my time as a homemaker to lay the foundation for what is now known as the Stonecroft Ministries.

Clearly, the Duff children were remarkable in their service to God. They were also remarkable in their influence on the generations that followed them. In Helen's case, her life impact was worldwide, and easily traceable to millions of lives through the work of Stonecroft Ministries.

The American and international cultures each changed on a dime throughout the 1960s, 70s, and 80s. The highly relational and non-judgmental approach of CWC and other Stonecroft initiatives offered just the right touch for many hundreds of thousands who might have otherwise been trapped in the culture around them.

The prime of Helen Baugh's life and ministry had come just at the right time: God's time.

Chapter 11

Twilight

One day Ruth, a Stonecroft staff worker, found Helen Baugh sitting quietly in back of the Stonecroft chapel. Helen seemed to be in deep contemplation, so Ruth turned away in hope that she wouldn't disturb her. Helen *had* noticed her, of course, and motioned for Ruth to sit next to her. Helen looked around the chapel again and spoke quietly, as if in awe.

"Ruth, isn't this chapel beautiful? I can't believe what God has done."

Ruth nodded her agreement. She stayed in the chapel a few more moments until Helen rose to leave, then walked her to the door.

Later Ruth remarked to a friend, "I'm not sure Mrs. Baugh understands the impact she has all over the world."

Perhaps Ruth was right. Maybe that's why Helen was reluctant at first to receive the honorary doctorates Taylor University wanted to bestow on her and Mary Clark.

"This can't be right," Helen remarked when she opened the envelope that held the announcement. The letter announced the Board of Trustees of Taylor University "voted to confer an honorary doctorate upon you in recognition of the significant service you have rendered in the name of Jesus Christ in the larger Christian community … We are happy to be the Christian college to recognize you in this manner."

"I can't accept such an honor," Helen responded.

Her staff finally convinced her that she could.

So on February 23, 1981, Taylor University President Dr. Milo Rediger bestowed honorary doctorates to Helen and Mary with these words: "In view of the remarkable accomplishments of these exceptional women, and the good they have done for mankind, Taylor University is delighted to make Mrs. Baugh and Miss Clark honorary alumnae of Taylor University."

Helen was thrilled to be in the company of a new generation of Christian scholars and students. She simply beamed at seeing so many women from the Christian Women's Clubs in the area. Yet in response to the honor she had received, she always referred back to the Bible verse she memorized as a child, "Not unto us, O Lord, not unto us, but unto Thy name give glory, for Thy mercy, and for Thy truth's sake."

She meant it, too.

If anyone knew about the all-too-human quirks and failings of Helen Baugh, it was probably Helen Baugh. She knew she wasn't perfect, even when many around her treated her as though she were.

Helen knew that her powers of persuasion were just one small step away from being manipulative. She had to constantly be on guard that she was hearing God, and not the Irish in her, when she was negotiating.

Helen was a classic visionary. She dealt with the big picture issues, but she needed people like Mary Clark and cadres of capable co-laborers to handle details and logistics.

Helen agonized over being an absentee mother for years. The longer she was away from family life, the harder it became for her to concentrate on the details of family life. She often engaged ministry life as though it were family life—and in many ways, her functional family was her Stonecroft family.

That said, her children and their families kept their relationships with Helen intact by realizing that she was uniquely gifted and called by God to be who she was. And they loved her for it.

In fact, because Helen submitted herself to God just as she was each day, she had a remarkable life—flaws and all.

By the mid-1980s, health issues forced Helen to slow down. When Helen and Mary would speak somewhere, they often ended with a prayer request: "Please pray with us that the Lord would keep Mrs. Baugh's blood pressure up, and Miss Clark's down."

The request met with laughter, but the old proverb remained intact: In every jest lies a bit of truth.

The truth was, Helen was thinking about her retirement. She would travel when she could. She would speak occasionally. She would write some articles for the ministry. But she would slow down significantly.

In January 1989, just after 50 years of leadership with Stonecroft Ministries as Founder and National Chairman of Christian Business and Professional Women, Vice Chairman of Christian Women's Clubs of the United States and Canada and Village Missions, Helen formally announced her retirement. In response, the National Board members named Helen National Chairman Emeritus of Christian Business and Professional Women of America.

And, finally, Helen had to listen to how others appreciated her.

As one might expect, tributes poured in at the announcement of Helen's retirement.

Helen's brother and sister-in-law, Walter and Edith Duff, said, "Only eternity will reveal what this one selfless life, completely 'sold out' to God, has accomplished."

Don and Gladys Harding, who worked with Helen for 23 years, wrote, "Knowing Mrs. Baugh personally opens up a whole book on prayer and the secret of how to pray. It doesn't matter what time of the day or night it is, she is constantly on speaking terms with her God."

"Often I hear [Helen] say, 'I never look at an individual without wondering where they are going to spend eternity.' It was said of Jesus, '*He beheld the city, and wept over it*' (Luke 19:41). Mrs. Baugh has seeing eyes and a weeping heart, as He had," said Milllie Stamm, who worked over 30 years alongside Helen in Stonecroft's prayer ministry.

Ruth Peachey, a successful businesswoman who became Stonecroft's Chairman of the Board when Mrs. Baugh stepped down, reflected, "Wherever she goes, our Mrs. Baugh has an awareness of God and she instills that very awareness in each of us. Because of her assurance in the power of prayer, we become aware of the power of God—that indeed all things *are* possible."

Several testimonies made reference to Helen being one of the great leaders of her generation. Others noted her sly sense of humor.

"I just played a trick on Mary."

Helen had a twinkle in her eye as she made the announcement to the hospitality staff gathered in the Manor kitchen for a coffee break. She made a grand sweeping gesture toward the foyer. The staff made their way to the doorway leading to the foyer.

There were shoes, dozens of shoes, in a line that led up the staircase in one direction and out the front door in another.

"I always wondered how long the line would be if Miss Clark's shoes were placed in a line next to each other. I thought for years they would at least reach from her closet to downtown Kansas City. Sadly, I think they only made it to the driveway."

Helen chuckled and went to the kitchen to pour a cup of coffee. "Let's leave them where they are and see if Miss Clark recognizes them. I imagine there are shoes there she's forgotten about years ago."

Mary Clark, however, had already noticed the trail of shoes as she walked toward the Manor from the Stonecroft offices. "What?...How?.... *What are my shoes doing in the driveway?*"

It was Mary Clark, Helen's partner in ministry for four decades, whose comments brought a laser focus on the core of Helen's work. Addressing the Stonecroft family the evening of Helen's retirement Mary said,

"Because Mrs. Baugh is the founder of Stonecroft Ministries, there will never be another person like her. God implanted this ministry in her heart because she was of such simple, child-like faith. As God led her, she followed Him step by step—with no organization, no wealthy individual, or no influential religious leader backing her. Step by step, God used her to add to His kingdom and He brought person after person to join with her. He has blessed her ministry in a very unusual way.

"The Bible says, 'Where there is no vision, the people perish.' What is Mrs. Baugh's vision? Her vision is to reach people one by one. In the beginning, she had no desire for getting groups together, except for prayer, but by reaching one by one, the first Christian Business & Professional Women's Council began. That Council sent out their very first missionary—a missionary who would simply go around and talk to people about the Lord. One by one, the missionary outreach grew."

In fact, at the time of Helen Baugh's 1989 retirement, the ministry had grown to 100 fulltime missionaries on staff with tens of thousands of volunteers. The various Stonecroft ministry expressions combined touched literally millions of people annually.

After half a century of profoundly dedicated leadership, and winning thousands of people to a relationship with Jesus Christ one by one, Helen felt she could take the first steps toward resting from her labors.

Shortly after Helen Baugh retired, the Stonecroft staff gathered to celebrate her birthday. Helen offered a brief word of encouragement to those who surrounded her that evening: "Carry on for me. Carry on the one consuming passion of my life: reaching people for Jesus Christ. My desire is for God to use you in rerouting people to Heaven."

After she retired, Helen took great pleasure in stopping by the desks of Stonecroft staff members to just visit for awhile—something she rarely had time to do as the active chairman of the organization. This day she approached Jo who, with her late husband Duncan, had provided leadership for both the Couples' Clubs and the advent of computers in the Stonecroft offices.

"Honey, where is your beloved?"

Jo was understandably surprised at the question. She also knew that Mrs. Baugh would never tease about such an issue, so she formed her response accordingly. "Well, Mrs. Baugh, Duncan is in Heaven with your Elwood, and I think they're planning how to surprise us when we get there."

A start of recognition flashed across Helen's face. It was clear that Duncan's death was news to her, all over again. "Oh. Oh," she said, recovering. "I imagine they're having fun up there, don't you?"

Jo smiled and nodded. It was a moment poignant enough to make her cry, but she wouldn't let that happen in front of Mrs. Baugh. Not now.

"Where's my purse? Has anyone seen my purse?"

Helen was losing her purse a lot these days. "Mrs. Baugh, let's take your walk without your purse today. We'll stay on the grounds." Liz had taken care of Helen for several years now. Even when Mrs. Baugh couldn't place other people, she knew and trusted Liz.

"Let's go down to the highway, Liz."

Helen and Liz strolled to a point on the grounds that overlooked Interstate 435. It was a peaceful, almost idyllic, autumn day. Helen seemed entranced by the traffic. They stood in silence for a few minutes, then Helen spoke.

"Liz?"

"Yes'm."

Helen sighed. "Liz, all these people on the highway—where are all these people going when they die?"

Liz stood stunned, but for just a moment. *Mrs. Baugh may be losing some things,* she thought, *but she's surely holding on to her heart for God.*

Time passed. Helen became less communicative. Yet every day when she was able, she would put on a dress (no one at Stonecroft could remember seeing Mrs. Baugh in slacks—ever), a strand of pearls, and sit on the bench swing in front of the Manor.

The Stonecroft staff made it a point to stop by, even for a moment, to chat with Helen. There was always a twinkle in her eye, and somehow her Irish wit was able to shine through.

One afternoon a Stonecroft worker sat down on the swing beside Helen and began singing hymns to her. After a few hymns, the worker noticed Helen seemed deep in thought.

"Mrs. Baugh, may I ask what you're thinking?"

Helen paused just a moment. "Well, I'm thinking about your singing. It isn't very good."

Yet many times, people who had those quick chats with Helen walked away challenged and encouraged. One new staff member introduced herself to Helen, who responded, "Reaching people for the Lord is serious business, dear, but try to have fun doing it." Others remember Helen offering a Bible verse (or several) from memory, and the verse being pertinent to their lives that day. Still others remember pointed questions about their work on the field: "Now, honey, what do you think about when you're in the cities?" "What are you doing today for the Lord?" "Do you remember to hand out your LIFE booklets?"

Then there was the simple expectation that Helen held for her Stonecroft family when they brought up any issue. Helen's response in her later years was the same as it had been years before: "Honey, let's pray right now."

The years would melt away. Helen's awareness of God would instill that same awareness in her prayer partner in that moment, and things would somehow be different, be better, when they said "Amen" together.

When Helen would write about the death of a Christian, she would call it a "Homegoing." February 7, 1996, marked the Homegoing of Helen Duff Baugh. Tributes to Helen's integrity and leadership flooded in. Her memorial service was packed with people.

Mary Clark reminded those who knew and loved Helen of her last months on earth. "Mrs. Baugh let her light shine for Jesus. And if she could speak, do you know what she would say? 'Do you know Jesus? Have you received Him?' That's what she'd say. She said that to everybody she met. And then she would say, 'But what are you doing for Him?'"

Perhaps the greatest testimony to her life is that, even today, people accurately remember Helen Duff Baugh for who she was: a woman of prayer, an evangelist *extraordinaire*, and a sold-out follower of Jesus. Helen's had been a life well-lived; not devoid of heartache or perfect in any way, but well-lived. Out of her life came life for many countless others, one by one, rerouted to Heaven through an Irish preacher's daughter and her friends.

It's a legacy that continues to this day—and one worth pursuing.

Chapter 12

The Story Goes On

So, what about you? Are you a Helen Baugh for your generation? You just might be! The wonderful thing (and perhaps, the reassuring thing,) is that Helen was not a perfect icon. She was just a woman who let God take her talents and her flaws and do whatever He desired to do through her. Someone, maybe, such as you?

Let's look at what you might have in common with Helen. From her life, we can find elements that make great leaders for their generation.

» Helen was a person who prayed.

Are you willing to let God build you into one?

Helen wasn't a natural at prayer. She learned *techniques* for prayer from her parents, but she was an adult before prayer became a priority to her. What turned the corner for Helen was the realization that prayer mattered; listening to God mattered. She realized God wanted to communicate with *her.* She was willing to ask God and WAIT for His answer. She learned not to settle for second best. She was willing to pray with others and she expected God to answer.

- Are you willing to take time to pray?
- Do you expect God to answer your prayers?
- Are you willing to make prayer a priority in your life?

You can start small: Find *one* other person to become your prayer partner. Together, ask God, "Please make a way for us to share Jesus with the people around us, in a way they can receive." God wants to communicate with you. He wants to let you in on the plans He has for you. He wants to give you great ideas to reach the people around you with His love. It starts with **prayer**.

» Helen had great faith.

Are you willing to have your faith stretched?

Helen wasn't born with great faith. It grew in her as she watched those she loved trust God, and she learned He was faithful. She stepped out in faith and tried new things...and watched to see if God was part of it. She learned to ask God for big things—God-sized things that only He could accomplish. She was willing to step out of her comfort zone for the sake of going where God led her.

- Can you believe God wants to take you on a faith adventure? (He does!)
- What is the biggest thing you ever hoped God would do through you?
- Can you imagine He would like to do even more?

When God plants an idea in your heart, use your great resource, **prayer**, to see how it stacks up with God and His Word. Then, use your **faith** to step out and watch God accomplish God-sized things!

» Helen had a passion to tell others about Jesus.

Are you willing to have God build the heart of an evangelist into you?

Helen wasn't born with that passion, you know. It was built into her by watching her father as he used every opportunity to tell others about having a relationship with God. It grew in her as she used creative means to offer hope and the "good news" to others. More often than not, for Helen, there were NO pre-existing avenues for her evangelism. She created them! Helen found ways to meet the needs she discovered around her. When the way was blocked, she prayed and followed God forward, even if the way was unconventional. It didn't take as much creativity to do meetings in churches as it did to take a hurting girl to dinner to tell her about Jesus. She saw a need, and came up with a creative way to meet it. *God* made it grow.

- Can you do these things? Sure you can! Think about the people around you who don't know Jesus. What are the needs they have in their lives?
- What is one thing you can do to meet *one* of the needs you are aware of?
- Can you think of a new way to tell them about Jesus and His love for them, based on this need you know they have?

God is already crazy about the people around you who don't know Him. He will surely make a way for you to reach them with His love. Remember, it starts with **prayer**, and needs **faith** that God *wants to* and *can* do big things. Just watch the things He's going to do—through you!

You know, the story doesn't have to end here.

God needs leaders in *your* generation.

God needs leaders in *your* neighborhood.

God is ready to build you into a person who makes a huge impact on *your* world.

Because the future of God's work in our world looks a lot like *you*!

Are you willing?

Then this story is just beginning!

You can contact the people at Stonecroft Ministries for ideas and opportunities to reach out to people around you. They have Bible study resources, organized groups all around the world, and people of prayer ready to come alongside you as you begin your own adventure in faith. Here's how to reach them:

STONECROFT RESOURCE CENTER

P.O. Box 9969
Kansas City, Missouri 64134-0969
Phone: 1.800.525.8627
FAX: 816.763.5565
E-mail: resourcecenter@stonecroft.org

www.stonecroft.org

And then there is one more thing we need to cover before you close this book. Perhaps you might be like Helen's husband, Elwood—part of a church, but you never understood that you must *choose* to have a relationship with God. Or perhaps all this God stuff is new to you. We would be wrong (and Helen would be deeply disappointed!) if we didn't offer you the chance to "choose Jesus." So here's the Gospel in a nutshell:

God set up the universe with certain rules. One of those is that sin—our rebellion against Him, our wrong choices—has consequences. One of the consequences, and probably the worst, is that sin puts a barrier between us and God.

To pay for our sins, and knock down that barrier, would cost more than we could ever pay, even if we worked hard all our life, or for many lifetimes. God loved us enough that He didn't want to be separated from us. So, He paid the cost for our sins! It was as if Jesus stepped in front of us and said to God, "Wait! Don't punish them, punish me!" And so God laid all the sins of the world—including yours—on Jesus, on the cross. And when He died, so did God's anger against your sin. All was forgiven. The barrier had been overcome.

So, everything's taken care of, right? Well, yes…and no. Jesus' gift of taking care of your sin is just that—a *gift.* Unless you receive a gift, it isn't really yours. That is what Elwood discovered; he had never received Jesus' gift to him. He'd only acknowledged that it was there.

Today, you can receive from God the great gift He's given to you. Make it your own! If you are ready to do that, you can pray a prayer something like this one that Helen used to lead many people into their relationships with God:

"Dear Lord Jesus,

Thank you for giving Your life on the cross to take the punishment for my sin. I accept Your forgiveness of every sin I have ever committed.

Right now I turn from going my own way and I invite You to come into my life. I make my choice to live for You. I want to start having a real relationship with You now.

Thank you for the privilege of being born into God's family right now, and for Your gift of everlasting life."

If you prayed that prayer, Stonecroft has some materials they'd like to send you that can help you better understand what you've just done. They want to help you establish your relationship with Jesus in a positive way. To find out more, let them know about your new relationship today by contacting them at:

STONECROFT HOME OFFICE

P.O. Box 9609
Kansas City, Missouri 64134-0609
Phone: 1.800.525.8627
FAX: 816.763.5565
E-mail: connections@stonecroft.org

www.stonecroft.org